'TO FORCE THE ENEMY OFF THE SEA'

The Story of the RAF's North Coates
Strike Wing

John Vimpany
&
David Boyd

Helion & Company

Helion & Company Limited
Unit 8 Amherst Business Centre
Budbrooke Road
Warwick
CV34 5WE
England
Tel. 01926 499 619
Email: info@helion.co.uk
Website: www.helion.co.uk
Twitter: @helionbooks
Visit our blog at blog.helion.co.uk

Published by Helion & Company 2022
Designed and typeset by Mach 3 Solutions (www.mach3solutions.co.uk)
Cover designed by Paul Hewitt, Battlefield Design (www.battlefield-design.co.uk)

Front cover: 'The aircraft that 'forced them off the seas' – Beaufighters of
236, 143 and 254 Squadrons over North Coates 1944. (Painting by Robin
Smith G.Av.A reproduced by kind permission of the artist)

ISBN 978-1-80451-085-8

British Library Cataloguing-in-Publication Data
A catalogue record for this book is available from the British Library

For details of other military history titles published by Helion & Company Limited
contact the above address or visit our website: http://www.helion.co.uk.

We always welcome receipt of book proposals from prospective authors.

Contents

Memorial to the North Coates Strike Wing at Cleethorpes, Lincolnshire. (Photo: Darren Austin, Cleethorpes RAFA)

This memorial commemorates the men and women who served as pilots, navigators and ground personnel which formed the Royal Air Force North Coates Strike Wing during World War II. From 1942 to 1945 covering the coastal regions of Norway, Denmark, Germany, Holland, Belgium and France, from Bergen to the Skaggerak, the Frisian islands, the North Sea, the English Channel and the Bay of Biscay to Bordeaux.

Operating with Bristol Beaufighter aircraft armed with cannon, bombs, torpedo and rockets they inflicted heavy losses and damage to shipping, denying freedom of the sea for supply purposes for the Nazi German forces and war industry.

Over 150,000 tons of enemy shipping was destroyed. These attacks were made by day and night, flying at very low altitude in combat conditions of very heavy German anti-aircraft fire. 120 aircraft failed to return and 241 aircrew from Great Britain, the Commonwealth and our Allies gave their lives flying with the Royal Air Force North Coates Strike Wing (Nos 143, 236 and 254 Squadrons).

In 2021 the Memorial was restored by the Cleethorpes RAF Association, and a Service of Re-dedication and Remembrance held on 5 December 2021, led by the Chaplain of RAF Coningsby and attended by the Vice Lord-Lieutenant of Lincolnshire, the Mayor of Cleethorpes, and representatives from the Royal Air Force, Royal Canadian Air Force, and other organisations and members of the public.

Authors' Preface

John Vimpany

Why don't you turn it into a book? After years of postponing the study and organisation of the papers of my late father, Dick Vimpany, I had at last started to do so and was describing the material to my friend David Boyd. I had mentioned to him that I was minded to write a short Memoir of my father's time in the war to pass to my children, who showed an informed and sincere awareness of the events of 1939-45 and the part played by their grandfather's generation. David, an amateur historian whom I knew to be well-read on the Second World War, quickly carried out some desk research of his own into the role of Coastal Command's Strike Wings and became very interested.

From 1943 to 1945 my father was stationed at RAF North Coates in Lincolnshire and flew as a navigator on one of the three Strike Wing squadrons based there. David and I decided to expand our research into the Wing's place in the history of the air-sea war and a plan to co-author this book soon emerged. To give the historical narrative a more personal dimension, we would draw on my father's recollections and material. I hoped that this would reveal more about his experience and resonate with those of the thousands of other aircrew who flew and fought. Also, we would not forget the parts played by the many hundreds more who supported them on the ground.

I had never meaningfully discussed with my father his time 'in the war'. I had regarded his life in the RAF as just another job and had shown only polite but limited interest in his wartime service. But as I looked through his photographs of Strikes, letters, logbook, notes and other material, I realised that there was much that could be brought out and explored to throw light on what he and his fellow aircrew experienced. I so regret now that he and I never discussed this in proper depth, and that I never asked him to describe what he had actually done or how he felt at the time or later.

Like many of his contemporaries, he was generally silent on the subject unless asked. Like thousands of others, he had joined the wartime RAF not because he was 'excited by flying' or 'for a career' but solely to defeat the enemy. When asked by a researcher in the 1990s if the heavy casualties sustained by the Wing affected morale he replied, *We flew against the enemy convoys for one reason – to force them off the seas, which we did. Morale at North Coates was always good. There was sadness when our friends did not return, but we did as we were told.*

David Boyd

I had never heard of the Strike Wings until John first showed me his father's wartime papers and photographs. It quickly became clear that here was a fascinating and important campaign, that had not received the attention it deserved during the war, and has been overlooked subsequently by historians, with a very limited body of work produced compared to other areas of the conflict. We therefore set out to redress this imbalance.

We have sought to present a well-researched broad historical narrative, providing context and analysis alongside the human story of the North Coates Strike Wing, and avoiding unnecessary drama or sentimentality. Our aim has been to produce a book that is accessible, interesting and informative to any reader, regardless of their level of knowledge about the RAF or the campaigns of the Second World War.

It is nearly eighty years since the Wing flew out across the North Sea – that time has not dimmed what those young men achieved.

Hurst, Berkshire 2022

Acknowledgements

Many people have assisted us during the researching and writing of this book and our grateful thanks are due to all of them:

Brian Stafford was the long-serving Secretary of the North Coates Flying Club, is the historian of the former RAF station, and de facto curator of North Coates airfield as an historic site. Brian gave us full access to his unpublished manuscript 'From Bi-plane to Bloodhound', which has been a hugely valuable source of information, and has always responded generously to our many requests for help when researching the book. Also, his Flying Club colleagues have always made us welcome on our visits to North Coates, and the Club's members are clearly very conscious of their aviation heritage.

Sylvia Darby, now a centenarian, is proud to have served at North Coates as a WAAF during the war, and she very kindly contributed part of her own wartime memoir and several photographs. John D. Care, son of the late Strike Wing Torbeau pilot John Care DFC, allowed us to use items from his father's diary and records, including logbook information and photographs. The family of Freddie Gardiner DFC, Alex Gardner (step-daughter) and Mary Fleck (daughter) provided us with information about Freddie's life and career and allowed us to reproduce the Eric Kennington portrait.

Lee Barton of the RAF's Air Historical Branch gave freely of his time to search the AHB's photo archives and pull together a collection of Strike Wing and other photographs for us to use.

Nigel Gardner, post-war RAF Coastal Command (Shackleton) navigator, and former colleague and good friend of the late Dick Vimpany reviewed our work from an airman's perspective. (Any mistakes in RAF terminology or language must clearly remain the authors' responsibility!) Colin McCarthy, a retired professional cartographer, produced the bespoke maps to our ever-changing specification. Peter Shepherd read an early draft of the book and provided advice on its structure and style and Rob Hargreaves advised us on publishing issues. John Tuck of the North Coates Flying Club and Darren Austin of Cleethorpes RAFA took photographs for us at North Coates and Cleethorpes. Stuart Arundel farms what was once RAF Donna Nook and lent us his copy of Martin Plummer's history of that airfield.

Introduction

From the start of the Second World War it was clear to the British leadership that the supply of raw materials, in particular high grade iron ore from Scandinavia, would form a crucial element in Germany's ability to maintain its armaments production and keep its armies in the field. It was not until late 1942, however, that the RAF developed an effective offensive capability against the heavily defended German shipping convoys that carried iron ore and other industrial materials from Sweden and Norway into Rotterdam, from where it was taken by barge to feed the armaments factories in the Ruhr valley.

This new attacking threat came from Coastal Command's 'Strike Wings', based at airfields around Britain's northern and eastern seaboard, each one made up of two or three squadrons equipped with Bristol Beaufighters. These were strong and powerful twin-engine aircraft, capable of attacking ships with cannon, torpedoes, bombs and rockets, and able to absorb significant damage.

The first of these Strike Wings comprised 143, 236 and 254 Squadrons based at RAF North Coates in Lincolnshire, an airfield on the coast just south of Grimsby. From early 1943 until the end of the war in Europe in May 1945, the North Coates Wing attacked German shipping making its way along the coast of Holland. Losses of aircraft and crews were high, but so too were enemy sinkings, and by the late summer of 1944 the campaign had been won and the North Sea effectively closed to large scale German shipping.

This book describes the role and operations of the North Coates Strike Wing and the men who served on its squadrons in 1943–45, presenting a narrative of the Wing's operations alongside an analysis of the wider strategic context in which these took place; and always aiming to remember the men of the Strike Wing, and their aircraft, and the fierce war they fought over those two years.

The book begins by setting out the strategic challenge which the Allies faced in the North Sea, and the piecemeal response effected during the first three years of the war, when other threats and other theatres claimed a higher strategic priority. Inevitably this resulted in heavy loss of life among the anti-shipping crews, disproportionate to the results achieved against the German convoys, and by mid-1942 it had become clear to the High Command that a fresh approach was required.

The book then describes the changes in strategy and tactics that were introduced through the course of 1942, by the end of which the North Coates wing had been formed and equipped with Beaufighters. This is followed by descriptions of many of the anti-shipping Strikes launched from North Coates from April 1943 onwards, the numerous successes and occasional failures, with many ships sunk or damaged, but many lives lost too on both sides of the conflict, as the Strike Wings gained the upper hand against the German convoys. By the late summer of 1944 the enemy had effectively been driven off of the North Sea along the coast of Holland.

The backgrounds, careers, and activities of some of the men who flew in the North Coates Strike Wing are then briefly described, as well as the day-to-day life they led on the station, and in the local area.

Finally, the book considers the 'balance sheet' – the success of the anti-shipping campaign in general, and the North Coates Strike Wing in particular, in achieving the objective that they were set up to deliver – to sink German controlled merchant ships and, in doing so, to choke off the supply of iron ore and other war materials into Rotterdam.

A postscript describes the post-war history of North Coates, including its role as a front-line anti-aircraft missile base during the Cold War, and then its return to civilian life as a Flying Club, but not before the Wing's veterans visited again, in 1999, to unveil their memorial to the 241 comrades who had failed to return.

254 Squadron navigator Dick Vimpany, at the end of the war, aged 22. (Photo: Vimpany archive)

Dick Vimpany

Dick Vimpany joined the Royal Air Force Volunteer Reserve (RAFVR) in 1941 as an aircrew cadet, aged 18. After two years training, in May 1943 he was posted as a Navigator to 254 Squadron, flying Beaufighter torpedo bombers from North Coates airfield, on the North Sea coast.

Over the next fifteen months he flew on 45 operational sorties, including 11 successful Strikes on enemy convoys. His pilot on most of these operations was Squadron Leader Freddie Gardiner DFC, a Battle of Britain veteran, and together they led the Wing's torpedo bombers on a number of the successful Strikes mounted during this period. As well as Wing Strikes, Gardiner and Vimpany flew on many solo reconnaissance missions, two of which resulted in successful Wing Strikes. After resting at the end of his operational tour in 1944, Dick Vimpany returned to 254 Squadron as an intelligence officer and remained with the squadron until the end of the war in Europe.

Dick Vimpany left the RAF at the end of the war and spent six years flying commercial transport aircraft, including ferrying refugees in India after Partition, and carrying supplies during the Berlin airlift. Re-joining the RAF in 1952, he served in Ceylon and in Borneo during the 'confrontasi' with Indonesia, for which he was awarded the MBE. Retiring from the RAF in 1966 he spent 17 years as an operational scientist at the Aircraft Experimental Establishment at Boscombe Down. His story is described in more detail at the end of the book.

Dick Vimpany attended many of the North Coates Strike Wing reunions. He died in 2006. This book is dedicated to his memory.

Sources

RAF Coastal Command's anti-shipping campaign has been neglected by historians of the Second World War, certainly in comparison with the wealth of material produced about the Bomber and Fighter Command campaigns. This was also true of media coverage of the campaign during the war itself, when reporting about the activities of the RAF's anti-shipping units was rare. Newspapers and newsreels were dominated by the air battles fought in the skies above Britain and the bombing offensive over Germany, by the battle against the German U-boats in the Atlantic, and by the ebb and flow of the war in North Africa and then Italy. After June 1944, very understandably, the main focus of media attention was the progress of the war in North-West Europe. Compared to these immense campaigns, the small but fierce war waged by RAF Coastal Command against heavily armed German ships in the North Sea was a sideshow, for the media at the time and for historians later.

In producing this book, the authors have drawn on five main source areas. The first is the published work of military historians, of which the most comprehensive and important is that of Dr Christina Goulter, of the Department of Defence Studies at Kings College London and co-Director of the Sir Michael Howard Centre for the History of War. Published in 1995, her book *A Forgotten Offensive: Royal Air Force Coastal Command's Anti-Shipping Campaign, 1940-1945* is the definitive account of this subject. (Her interest in the anti-shipping campaign was influenced initially by her father's war-time service flying with a Strike Wing.) Another important historian is S.W Roskill, author of the magnificent three-volume official history, *The War at Sea* published between 1954-61, which covers many aspects of the anti-shipping campaign.

The second source are the published accounts by participants, drawing on their own personal experiences and those of fellow flyers. The most comprehensive of these is Roy Conyers Nesbit's *The Strike Wings 1942-45*, first published in 1984. Nesbit flew in an anti-shipping squadron during the first half of the war, later moving to the Far East. Although he was not involved directly during the period that his book covers, he draws heavily on the recollections of more than thirty Strike Wing aircrew, as well as British and German official records. The result is a wide-ranging and very readable account of the overall anti-shipping campaign from 1942 onwards. A number of other books about Coastal Command and the Beaufighter aircraft were also consulted – a full bibliography is included at the end.

The third major source are the official records of the units concerned. These are held in the National Archives and include the Operations Records Books (ORB) for the three squadrons comprising the North Coates wing (in the AIR 27 series), as well as that of RAF North Coates (AIR 28 series). An additional source (in the AIR 15 series) are the Dispatches written by each Commander-in-Chief of Coastal Command, the Command's monthly Reviews, and other papers covering anti-shipping strategy and tactics. These provide invaluable background about the strategic challenges and resource constraints faced.

Unpublished personal papers form the fourth source of material for the book. The most significant are those of the late Dick Vimpany of 254 squadron, now in the possession of his son, the co-author. As well as his logbook and photographs, these records include marked up squadron rolls and notes made in the margins of other books, including Nesbit's. He also wrote a short account of his experiences for use by a historical researcher. Another useful source is the logbook of John Care of 254 squadron, along with his contemporary diary entries and newspaper clippings, made public and used with the kind permission of his son, John D. Care. Valuable insights into life on the ground at North Coates was the memoir written by Sylvia Darby, who served as a WAAF at North Coates during the Strike Wing period, used by kind permission of her family.

The fifth source is a full history of North Coates, *From Bi-plane to Bloodhound* by Brian Stafford of the North Coates Flying Club. This major body of work is a detailed record of the day-to-day activities at the airfield, including during the Strike Wing period in 1943-45, and the authors are very grateful to Brian for allowing them access to this unpublished material.

Glossary

The following abbreviations are used throughout the book:

F/Sgt.	Flight Sergeant
P/O	Pilot Officer
F/O	Flying Officer
F/Lt.	Flight Lieutenant
S/Ldr.	Squadron Leader
W/Cdr.	Wing Commander
Gp/Capt.	Group Captain
DSO	Distinguished Service Order
DFC	Distinguished Flying Cross
DFM	Distinguished Flying Medal
WAAF	Women's Auxiliary Air Force
Flak	Anti-aircraft fire
M/V	Merchant Vessel

1

The Challenge

A supply of high-grade iron ore was essential for steel production in Germany, and the mines of northern Sweden were the only substantial source of this raw material in Europe. The iron ore mined in Sweden was exported to Germany along two routes. In the summer, when the sea was not frozen, ore could be shipped across the Baltic from the Swedish port of Lulea to ports along the northern coast of Germany. During the rest of the year, however, all of the ore had to be transported along a second route. This involved the ore being taken by rail to the northern Norwegian port of Narvik, from where it was carried down the shipping lanes along the coast of Norway, then across to Denmark, and down the Danish east coast to northern Germany.

Germany's industrial heartland, where its steel industry was concentrated, and so the main centre of demand for high-grade iron ore, was in the Ruhr valley. Although iron ore could be shipped along inland waterways from ports in northern Germany, the fastest way to get large quantities of this material into the Ruhr was by ship through the Kiel Canal and then down the Dutch coast to the port of Rotterdam, from where it went by barge to the steel plants in the Ruhr.

Germany's conquest of Norway, Denmark and the Netherlands in April and May 1940 gave it control over its iron ore supply routes, as well as bringing a substantial number of additional merchant ships under German control. The occupation of these countries also helped Germany to maintain pressure on Sweden to honour the commercial agreements it had entered into before the war, thereby ensuring the continuing supply of iron ore and other raw material supplies. These arrangements included the use of Swedish ships to carry significant tonnages of that country's raw material exports, and it was estimated that at times Swedish ships carried around half of all of the iron ore exported from Scandinavia.[1] These ships returned to Sweden carrying the coal and coke from Germany on which Sweden's own economy depended.

Britain had always been aware of the importance of Swedish iron ore to the German armaments industry, but all pre-war planning had assumed

---

1   Slessor Dispatch, The National Archives (TNA) AIR 15/773.

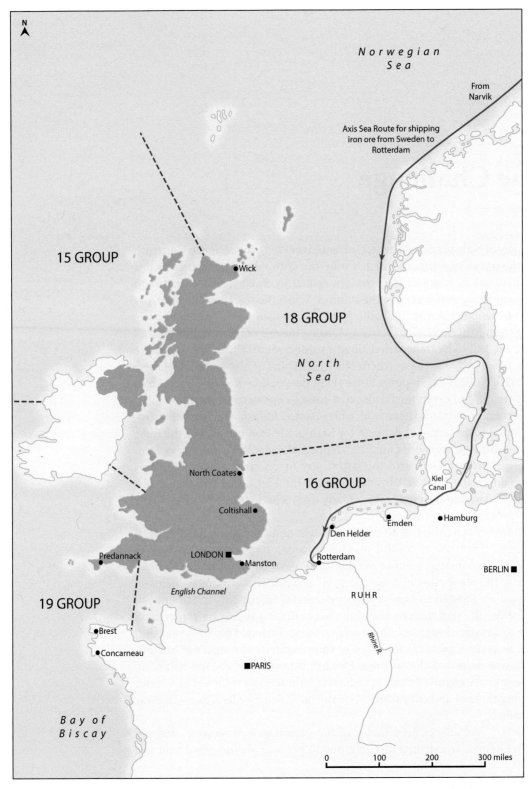

Coastal Command – North Sea/Channel Theatre, 1943-45. (Information sourced from Dennis Richards, *Royal Air Force 1939-1945, Vol. I, The Fight at Odds*)

that the Royal Navy would impose a blockade on Germany, as it had done during the First World War. However, a shortage of British naval resources available to enforce a blockade, and the Germans' ability after mid-1940 to base ships and aircraft in the territories it had invaded and occupied, meant that other options had to be explored. So the challenge of attacking the ships carrying iron ore to Germany was handed to the RAF, and specifically to an unprepared and under-resourced Coastal Command.

The wider picture

By the late summer of 1940, most of western Europe was under German control. In the east, Hitler's non-aggression pact with the Soviet Union had removed the threat to Germany from that quarter. In the south, Italy's late entry into the war was extending Axis control around the Mediterranean. The United States was a friendly trading partner for the UK but remained firmly neutral. Britain therefore stood alone, supported only by the Dominions and by the resources of its Empire, with no immediate prospect of help arriving from any other quarter.

The country's first priority was survival, against the threat of an invasion across the Channel and the threat of starvation if Germany closed the Atlantic shipping lanes, as had nearly happened in 1917. The prospect of invasion receded after the Battle of Britain, but this was succeeded by a German bombing campaign by night against British cities, and the escalation of the U-boat campaign against the merchant ships keeping the country supplied with the food, oil and raw materials it needed to survive. There was also the ever-present threat of a break-out by the big German capital ships to further threaten British merchant shipping. Away from British shores, Italian incursions into Greece and North Africa, supported later by Germany, threatened Britain's lines of communication with India and Australasia and their men and materials, and these too had to be protected.

Britain was therefore firmly on the defensive through the winter of 1940-41 and for the following year, deploying its limited resources to try to cope with the multiple threats both to the country itself and to its strategically important communications and supply lines. In this context, it is clear that developing and launching an effective offensive against German merchant ships in the North Sea was going to be a tall order.

2

The Response, 1940-42

A slow and costly start

Despite the desperate strategic situation which the country faced from 1940 to 1942, it is difficult to review the first three years of Britain's anti-shipping campaign without feeling that opportunities were wasted and lives needlessly lost. There was no consistent strategy, the resources deployed were inadequate, with aircraft used that were not suitable for the roles they were tasked to undertake, operational planning was haphazard, tactics were not thought through properly, and aircrew training was the minimum required to keep the squadrons manned and operational.

The results were predictable, with the rate of aircrew losses in anti-shipping squadrons among the highest of any service in any theatre in the whole war. In 1941 average losses on anti-shipping sorties were over 20 percent, and the probability of a torpedo bomber crew surviving a first tour of operations was calculated officially to be 17.5 percent. The surviving crew's chance of getting to the end of its second tour was just 3 percent,[1] and more than 600 Coastal Command aircraft were lost in the three years to the end of 1942.[2] Crews continued to go out on what they regarded as suicide missions, with those who survived prone to mental breakdown, when they would be at risk of being deemed as 'LMF', short for 'Lacks Moral Fibre', the official term for cowardice. Commanders who resisted orders to send their crews on these missions were sacked.[3]

Coastal Command's anti-shipping campaign of 1940–42 must be judged a failure in terms of the results achieved and the losses sustained. Individual heroism and perseverance did see more than a hundred German merchant ships sunk or damaged by all arms of the RAF during this period, but these numbers were not sufficient to justify the scale of losses sustained by the attackers. German convoys continued to sail into Rotterdam, and deliveries

---

1   Christine J.M. Goulter, *A Forgotten Offensive, Royal Air Force Coastal Command's Anti-Shipping Campaign, 1940-45* (Abingdon: Frank Cass & Co. Limited, 1995), p.155.
2   Roy Conyers Nesbit, *The Strike Wings*, (London: HMSO, 1995), p.20.
3   Arthur Aldridge with Mark Ryan, *The Last Torpedo Flyers* (London: Simon & Schuster, 2013), p.75.

of raw materials into the industrial complex of the Ruhr valley continued at pre-war levels.[4] By 1942 it was clear to all those involved, at all levels, that the anti-shipping campaign could not continue as it had done for the previous two years. There needed to be major change.

Campaign problems

Strategic priorities

Coastal Command began the war as the poor relation of the higher profile and more glamorous Fighter and Bomber Commands, and almost an afterthought in the RAF's resource planning and allocation. There was frequent friction between Coastal Command and Bomber Command, with turf wars fought over the roles and responsibilities of each, as well as who got the aircraft, ordnance and crews that became available. As the country started to be able to move away from the purely defensive, after the entry into the war of Russia in June 1941 and of the US in December of that year, the primary offensive campaign planned was the strategic bombing of Germany's industrial centres, and this subsequently absorbed the lion's share of Britain's available resources.

One factor in Coastal Command's favour was that although part of the RAF, its priorities were largely directed by the Admiralty, and in the early part of the campaign this helped to ensure that Coastal Command remained in existence as a fighting force. However, within the Admiralty, and therefore also Coastal Command, the anti-shipping campaign was well down the list of strategic priorities. Top of the list was the anti-submarine campaign, as Germany's U-boat wolf packs launched increasingly successful attacks on Britain's Atlantic supply lifeline. Coastal Command aircraft and crews were deployed primarily to provide cover for these convoys, as well seek out and attack the U-boats making their way from their base ports out into the Atlantic. In 1942 more than half of all Coastal Command operational sorties were anti-submarine patrols.[5]

For the squadrons that were allocated to anti-shipping duties, the first priority was to be ready to attack any German capital ships that ventured out of port to threaten Britain's Atlantic or Arctic convoys. The Admiralty saw these ships as a major strategic threat, to be penned into their bases and attacked at every opportunity. Enemy merchant ships were a secondary target, to be attacked when the opportunity arose and resources were available, rather than as part of a sustained campaign to damage Germany's raw material supply lines.

Coastal Command's Air Officer Commanding until June 1941, Air Chief Marshall Sir Frederick 'Ginger' Bowhill, summed up in his Dispatch the situation he faced: *Shortage of aircraft and aerodromes made the task of my Command in the early days of the war very difficult ... Offensive operations were thus subsidiary to the primary role of reconnaissance.*

---

4   Goulter, *A Forgotten Offensive*, p.354, Table 4
5   Coastal Command Review, AIR 15/470, December 1942.

The Dispatch written by Bowhill's successor, Air Chief Marshall Philip Joubert de la Ferté, in post from June 1941 until February 1943, made clear Coastal Command's strategic priorities for any offensive anti-shipping operations:

1   Attacking enemy surface warships and U-boats
2   Launching torpedo attacks in enemy harbours
3   When no naval targets presented themselves, bombing attacks on enemy merchant shipping outside the area from Cherbourg to Texel.[6]

The geographic constraints imposed on Coastal Command's potential offensive operations against enemy merchant shipping was due to the area between Cherbourg and Texel, which is the mainland European coastline closest to Britain, having been reserved solely for Bomber Command attacks. Joubert also made clear that the aircraft under his command had to *reserve torpedoes for worthwhile targets*.

Aircraft and crews

The lowly status of Coastal Command was reflected in the aircraft made available to it through the 1940–42 period. The main bombing force consisted of Hudsons, which had originally been designed as a civil airliner, sometimes reinforced by Blenheims seconded from Bomber Command. Both were sturdy but slow, relatively lightly armed, vulnerable to flak when operating at low level, and therefore unsuitable for a maritime strike role.

The primary torpedo bomber in use was the Beaufort, another sturdy but under-powered twin-engine aircraft with a crew of four, made up of pilot, navigator, wireless operator, and gunner. A popular aircraft with some crews, and an effective torpedo bomber in other theatres later in the war, its major disadvantage was its lack of speed and manoeuvrability.

Lockheed Hudson – sturdy but slow and lightly armed. (Photo: Lockheed Corporation)

---

6   Joubert Dispatch, The National Archives (TNA) AIR 15/773

Bristol Blenheim – RAF 'all-rounder' but no match for single-engine fighters. (Photo: Crown Copyright/Air Historical Branch)

Some Hampden bombers were adapted for torpedo bombing but these aircraft were already becoming out-dated and were too slow for torpedo bombing attacks during daylight, although they did enjoy some success by night off the Norwegian coast. None of these aircraft was sufficiently well-armed or fast enough to take on or outrun German fighters.

Aircraft serviceability was a significant problem across all of the RAF but particularly in Coastal Command, which had last call on resources. At times, the Command's aircraft availability dipped as low as 40 percent, compared to an average of 70 percent across the rest of the RAF.[7] This meant that even when tasked to mount operations in force, the squadrons could not put all of their aircraft into the air.

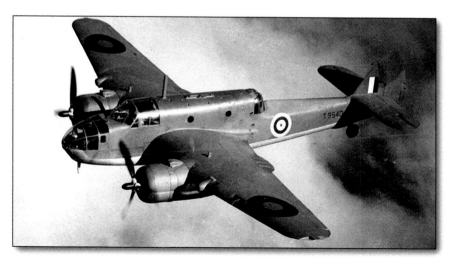

Bristol Beaufort – under-powered and cumbersome – Coastal Command's main torpedo bomber until mid-1942. (Photo: Crown Copyright/ Air Historical Branch)

7   Goulter, *A Forgotten Offensive*, p. 132

Training establishments struggled to provide crews to fill the gaps caused by the losses sustained. This was the case for navigators and wireless operators as well as pilots, and at times the training units were turning out fewer than half the number of replacements required. The situation was exacerbated by the best recruits often being creamed off by Bomber Command. This was so serious that in February 1941 all offensive action against enemy merchant shipping had to be suspended temporarily, due to the shortage of available operational aircraft.[8]

Planning and Tactics

Coastal Command struggled to develop effective anti-shipping tactics using either conventional bombing or torpedo bombing. Towards the end of the First World War the RAF and Admiralty had developed successful anti-shipping tactics, using both bombs and torpedoes. By the start of the Second World War those lessons had been largely forgotten. In particular, it took time for the effectiveness of torpedo bombing to become recognised, and much of the early focus of the anti-shipping campaign was on bombing tactics. This situation was exacerbated by the shortage of torpedoes made available to Coastal Command.

When pressed home by resolute crews, low level bombing could be effective against ships, with up to 20 percent of attacks recording hits, but it led to high losses from flak. High level bombing was safer for the crews, but hits were rarely achieved, with a success rate of only 1 percent when the bombs were dropped from 4,000 feet.[9] Torpedo bombing was most effective if these were dropped at close range, ideally less than 1,000 yards, and from a height of around 150 feet. However, this exposed the attacker to the full force of the flak defences of a merchant ship and its escorts. Torpedo attacks had the highest probability of success if a group of torpedoes were dropped at the roughly same time, making it harder for the target ships to take avoiding action by turning away and presenting a narrower target. Aircraft and crew shortages meant that this was rarely possible, and torpedo attacks tended to be carried out by aircraft operating in twos and threes, or even singly. Even when a crew managed to push through the flak and launch its torpedo at the right height and range, frequently there were no hits scored.

Reconnaissance and intelligence were often hit-or-miss affairs. When reconnaissance patrols spotted potential targets, or other intelligence was received about a ship or convoy, sorties would be mounted against these, sometimes in strength. Even in this situation there were numerous instances of the attackers failing to find the target ship or convoy. Most torpedo operations were opportunistic 'rovers', in which two or three Beauforts would patrol the shipping lanes, hoping to spot a target that they could attack, before they themselves were found and attacked by enemy fighters. Losses from these sorties were kept down by operating as far as possible when there was low cloud over the Dutch coast that provided cover for the attack if a target was found and allowed a rapid withdrawal into the clouds afterwards.

8   Bowhill Dispatch, The National Archives (TNA) AIR 15/773
9   Coastal Command Review, AIR 15/470 Nov-Dec, 1942

Attacks by any of Coastal Command's units carried out without fighter cover left the attackers vulnerable to German fighters. These operated from airfields all along the coast of occupied Europe and could quickly get into the air to intercept Coastal Command's attacks or opportunistic patrols. When Fighter Command did provide cover for anti-shipping operations, frequently there were communications problems which meant that the rendezvous between the fighters and the strike force was missed. The slowness of the torpedo bombers and the height at which they operated also hampered the effectiveness of the fighter escorts, making them too vulnerable to the enemy fighters.

Gradual improvements evident

All of the problems described above were recognised at the time, and changes made to try to improve the effectiveness of the anti-shipping operations and reduce the level of losses. Lessons were being learnt the hard way, but they were being learnt and, importantly, they were being applied – when the resources were available.

The introduction of new aircraft did not begin effectively until the second half of 1942, when the anti-shipping squadrons had been equipped with the Beaufighter (about which much more later). However, from late 1940 onwards there was a major expansion of the training establishment, with new training units set up, including a torpedo training centre in Scotland as well as flying training schools in Canada and South Africa. Increasing the number of recruits to these centres was achieved by a combination of lowering the medical and educational requirements for aircrew, re-assessing ground crew to find potential airmen, and increasing the number of volunteers accepted from the army.

Another important development was the establishment by Coastal Command of an Operational Research section, manned by academics and other technical experts, tasked to analyse the data coming back from the front line and to find better ways of doing things. Aircraft availability was improved by instituting a system of 'planned flying and maintenance' at Wing level, combining the resources of several squadrons that operated from the same airfield and enabling prioritisation of work and more efficient use of people, equipment and spare parts. Operational reports were assessed, and crews questioned to find out which tactics worked and which failed, and why, and the results were communicated widely, including down to front-line units.

One of the channels used for the dissemination of information was the monthly Coastal Command Review, circulated to stations. These contained summaries of each of the areas of activity undertaken by the Command, such as anti-submarine, photo reconnaissance and anti-shipping. Operations were described and analysed in considerable detail, and individual actions highlighted. There was an emphasis on good news, rather than operational setbacks, but the Reviews contained little pure propaganda, which the readers on the front line would not have found credible. In addition, there were 'specialist and general' articles, dealing with subjects like navigation, photography, and escaping from a ditched aircraft. (There were also a surprising number of articles and photographs about the types and behaviours of the whales that could be encountered in the oceans covered by Coastal Command aircraft – there were occasions when diving whales had been attacked by aircraft, the crew believing them to be submarines!)

The role of intelligence began to increase, with more information about ships and convoys received from sources within the occupied territories, backed up by more aerial reconnaissance and better interpretation and analysis of this. Although highly secret at the time, it was in late 1941 that intelligence from the Enigma code-breaking programme began to become available, allowing information gained from other sources to be corroborated, and enabling a more accurate picture to be assembled of both enemy shipping movements and the impact of the campaign on German shipping.

Gradually therefore the anti-shipping campaign was becoming more effective. In the last three months of 1941, fifteen enemy merchant ships were sunk, a total of 45,000 tons, and ten damaged, for the loss of nineteen crews.[10] Losses were still high, but well down from the peaks of 1940–41. More aircraft were serviceable, better trained new crews were available, and more was known in advance about the movement of German shipping.

Then backwards again

However, the low strategic priority of Coastal Command's anti-shipping campaign continued to be demonstrated, when some of its newest aircraft and most experienced units were transferred to other theatres deemed to be more important. At a stroke Coastal Command lost a large proportion of its anti-shipping offensive capability. At the start of 1942 there were only three Beaufort squadrons left in Britain.[11]

In his Dispatch, Air Chief Marshall Joubert describes the arrival of Beaufighters into his Command in 1941, only for them to be sent overseas almost immediately. In August 1941 he lost 30 Beaufort crews and 24 Beaufighter crews, all posted to the Middle East theatre.[12] But his approach was clear, that while continually trying to get more resources for his Command, *we must do the best we can with the aircraft we have got.*

Many of Coastal Command's Beauforts ended up in Malta, where they took part in the successful campaign against the ships supplying Rommel's Afrika Corps. Those aircraft undoubtedly played a major role in the victories achieved in North Africa in 1942 and 1943; but the departure of a large part of its torpedo bombing force was a major step backwards for Coastal Command and its anti-shipping war. This was reflected in an increase in both accidents and operational losses, inevitable as the experienced crews were replaced by new, raw recruits.

10 Goulter, *A Forgotten Offensive*, p.147
11 S.W. Roskill, *The War at Sea, Vol. II* (London: HMSO, 1954-1961) p.165
12 Joubert Dispatch, (TNA) AIR 15/773

The enemy too was not standing still. In response to the RAF's early torpedo and bombing attacks, from the end of 1940 the Germans had implemented a convoy system for its merchant shipping. By 1942 these convoys had become better defended, with more escorts deployed, equipped with considerably more firepower to bring to bear against attacking aircraft. In mid-1942, daylight attacks on convoys were suspended again, due to the high casualty rates suffered by units pressing home low-level bombing attacks in Blenheim and Hudson aircraft – a quarter of the aircraft dispatched on operations in June failed to return.[13] Joubert was very honest in his dispatch *The Germans gradual increase in flak armament had won a temporary victory.*

As some of the participants saw it

An airman who recorded his participation in the 1940–41 campaign was Beaufort pilot Patrick Gibbs, who ended the war with a DSO and two DFCs. Gibbs was a hard-driving and sometimes controversial leader who later led the successful anti-shipping operations in Malta, developing tactics there that influenced the later North Sea campaign. In his books, written at the time, he describes the exploits of the Beaufort crews over the North Sea in 1940 and early 1941 as *indescribably gallant* but concludes that his squadron *lost its little war* with him being a *lonely survivor* who had the good fortune to be in hospital recovering from injuries during the winter months when losses were heaviest. When he returned to North Coates after leaving hospital, only one crew remained from when he had first joined the squadron. His book captures the 'devil may care' courage of the torpedo bombing crews, but behind the gung-ho attitude he describes, Gibbs fails to hide the pain he felt as his friends and colleagues were killed one by one. After leaving Malta in late 1942, Gibbs participated in Strike Wing tactical development conferences, and was briefly posted to command 254 Squadron at North Coates in early 1943. However, he never took up the appointment, as he was by then mentally and physically exhausted and received a medical discharge from the RAF in 1944.

Another important first-hand account of this period was written in 2013 by Beaufort pilot Arthur Aldridge, who won two DFCs, and his gunner Bill Carroll. Their book too reflects the superficially casual attitude to death that prevailed in their anti-shipping squadron, and the fatalistic approach with which crews approached each sortie. Carroll tells of the tradition in the Sergeants' mess that when a man was killed the money in his locker would be used to buy drinks in the mess. Returning late from one operation, after an emergency landing at another airfield, Carroll found his messmates using his money to toast his memory – and his immediate reaction was that at least there was enough money left for him to have a few drinks too!

---

13   Chris Ashworth, *RAF Coastal Command 1936-69* (London: Patrick Stephens, 1992) p. 60.

Feats of Valour, 1940-42

The story of Coastal Command's anti-shipping campaign before 1943 was not one entirely made up of losses and setbacks. The courage and determination of the crews (cited by the leading historian of the campaign as being *the only assets the Command had*)[14] enabled some notable successes against German merchant shipping, but *courage is not enough*.[15]

Patrick Gibbs flew with 22 Beaufort Squadron from late 1940 until mid-1941, when it was based at North Coates alongside 42 Squadron, also flying Beauforts. Many operations were mounted against German shipping making its way down the Dutch coast to Rotterdam, and a number of ships were sunk and damaged by crews from these two Beaufort squadrons. Arthur Aldridge flew his first operation with 217 Beaufort Squadron, based in Cornwall, in September 1941. In December they had been transferred to Manston in Kent and Aldridge flew one of the three Beauforts which sank an 8,000 ton German auxiliary liner off the Dutch coast.

Two Coastal Command operations during this period are worthy of particular mention:

Kenneth Campbell VC
The first of these epitomised the raw courage and absolute determination demonstrated by torpedo bomber crews against overwhelming odds, and the cost in terms of loss of life. Ken Campbell had been flying Beauforts with Patrick Gibbs on 22 Squadron since September 1940, mainly operating out of North Coates. He had achieved a number of successful torpedo strikes, sinking a merchant ship off Borkum in March 1941, and damaging another several days later near Ijmuiden.

In April 1941 Campbell's was one of six Beauforts ordered to mount a dawn attack against the German battleships *Scharnhorst* and *Gneisenau* which were lying in Brest harbour. High level bombing raids on these two formidable warships had been unsuccessful, and a torpedo attack was now ordered. Three of the Beauforts were carrying mines, and were to attack first, to destroy the torpedo nets and flak ships. The second wave, including Campbell, were then to go in for a close-range torpedo attack.

Brest was one of the most heavily defended facilities on the German-occupied Atlantic coast, home to U-boat pens and repair docks as well as the two battleships. It was estimated that there were as many as 1,000 anti-aircraft guns deployed against possible air attack. In his Dispatch, Air Chief Marshall Bowhill, who issued the order for the operation, described it as *one of the most desperate attacks that could possibly be conceived*.

The weather was poor and the aircraft became separated. Campbell arrived first, and after a period waiting for the others to appear he decided to press on alone. The citation for his Victoria Cross, awarded posthumously, best describes the event:

---

14   Christine J.M. Goulter, in *Royal Air Force Historical Society Journal*, Issue 33, 2005, p.27.
15   Nesbit, *The Strike Wings*, Chapter 2.

This officer was the pilot of a Beaufort aircraft of Coastal Command which was detailed to attack an enemy battle cruiser in Brest Harbour at first light on the morning of 6th April 1941. The aircraft did not return but it is known that a torpedo attack was carried out with the utmost daring.

The battle cruiser was secured alongside the wall on the north shore of the harbour, protected by a stone mole bending around it from the west. On rising ground behind the ship stood protective batteries of guns. Other batteries were clustered thickly round the two arms of land which encircle the outer harbour. In this outer harbour near the mole were moored three heavily armed anti-aircraft ships, guarding the battle cruiser. Even if an aircraft succeeded in penetrating these formidable defences, it would be almost impossible, after delivering a low-level attack, to avoid crashing into the rising ground beyond.

This was well known to Flying Officer Campbell who, despising the heavy odds, went cheerfully and resolutely to the task. He ran the gauntlet of the defences. Coming in at almost sea level, he passed the anti-aircraft ships at less than mast-height in the very mouths of their guns and skimming over the mole launched a torpedo at point-blank range.

The battle cruiser was severely damaged below the waterline and was obliged to return to the dock whence she had come only the day before. By pressing home his attack at close quarters in the face of withering fire on a course fraught with extreme peril, Flying Officer Campbell displayed valour of the highest order.

Flying Officer Kenneth Campbell – Beaufort pilot awarded posthumous Victoria Cross for his successful attack on German battleships in Brest harbour, April 1941. (Photo: Crown Copyright)

The other crew members, Sergeants Scott, Mulliss and Hillman were also killed. All were buried by the Germans with full military honours. Today, the main road running through the former base area at North Coates is named after Kenneth Campbell VC.

Flight to Paris

In the summer of 1942 the tide of war was still flowing against the Allies: mainland Europe all remained firmly under German control, and the Germans were launching large-scale offensive operations on the eastern front; the U-boats had the upper hand in the Atlantic and Britain's vital maritime supply line was precarious; in North Africa, Rommel was pushing the Eighth Army back into Egypt; and in the Far East, Singapore had fallen to the Japanese and the British army was in full retreat through Burma towards the Indian border. Optimism was in short supply, and any high profile actions that boosted morale were to be welcomed, however insignificant they were to the actual prosecution of the war.

Coastal Command provided one such gesture, using a Beaufighter and crew from 236 Squadron based at North Coates. This unit had received its first Beaufighters in March of that year, replacing the Blenheims with which it had previously been equipped.

Intelligence reports had been received that the German garrison in Paris paraded on the Champs Elysees every day at 12:15 p.m. It was also known that the Paris headquarters of the German Navy was close by. The Air Officer Commanding Coastal Command decided to send a Beaufighter to strafe the German parade and the Naval headquarters and drop a tricolour over the Arc de Triomphe. The new Beaufighter had the speed and the range for a low-level flight to Paris and back.

The experienced 236 Squadron crew of Flight Lieutenant Ken Gatward and his navigator Sergeant George Fern were 'asked to volunteer' and, of course, they did. After much practice, and several false starts due to poor weather, on 12 June 1942 Gatward and Fern took off in heavy rain from RAF Thorney Island near Portsmouth at 11:30 a.m. in their Beaufighter. An hour later, despite a bird strike en route, they were flying down the Champs Elysees. The intelligence about the parade was false, but everything else went to plan. Gatward's laconic log-book entry sums up the operation:

Paris – No cover – 0 ft. Drop Tricolours on Arc Triomphe & Ministry Marine. Shoot up German HQ. Little flak, no E.A. Bird in STBD oil radiator. Returned Northolt and on to Command. 61 photos. Heavy rain over England. France fair to light. Northolt to Thorney, Thorney return base.[16]

(EA: Enemy Aircraft; STBD: Starboard)

The raid was a propaganda triumph, as well as a demonstration of the qualities of the Beaufighter, and Gatward was awarded a DFC and Fern a DFM. After the raid Gatward had a one-year break from operations but returned to the anti-shipping campaign in mid-1943 and successfully led one of the Beaufighter squadrons in the Strike Wing based at Wick until the

The Paris skyline photographed by Gatward and Fern from their Beaufighter on 12 June 1942. (Photo: Crown Copyright/Air Historical Branch)

end of the war. George Fern later served as Station Navigation Officer at RAF North Coates.

The 'Channel Dash' in February 1942

One high profile incident in early 1942 highlighted the inadequacy of the resources available for offensive action in the English Channel and North Sea. The German battle-cruisers *Scharnhorst* and *Gneisenau* had been in Brest since the previous March. While there, they had been the targets of repeated air raids, including the torpedo attack by 22 Squadron's Kenneth Campbell. Both ships, along with the heavy cruiser *Prinz Eugen*, which was also in Brest, had suffered extensive damage and spent the second half of 1941 undergoing major repairs.

In January 1942, however, all three ships were once again fully operational and Hitler ordered them to move up to Kiel, for deployment in northern waters, where they could threaten the convoys now carrying aid to Russia. The German naval high command therefore laid plans for a surprise 'dash' up the Channel.

The Admiralty was aware that the ships were now ready for sea and that a break-out from Brest was probable in the near future, with a move up the Channel seen as the most likely route for the Germans to take. Preparations were made to intercept them: a flotilla of motor torpedo boats (MTB) and six destroyers were put on standby off north Kent; the few available minelayers and submarines were sent to sea; six Fleet Air Arm Swordfish armed with torpedoes were transferred to Manston in Kent; and No. 42 Squadron with fourteen Beaufort torpedo bombers was brought south to Norfolk. This was all in addition to the aircraft already in place, including Beaufort squadrons on the south and east coasts, a dozen Hudsons based in Norfolk, and more than 200 heavier bombers at various airfields around the east coast of England.

The three capital ships and their escorting destroyers left Brest just before midnight on 11 February and began to make their way up the Channel at a rapid twenty-seven knots. Poor weather and a series of reconnaissance mishaps meant that they were not spotted until noon on 12 February, nearly twelve hours later, by which time they were approaching the Straits of Dover.

Strikes were hurriedly ordered, and during the afternoon of 12 February the ships were attacked in piecemeal fashion by the naval Swordfish, by several groups of Coastal Command Beauforts and Hudsons, by RAF heavy bombers, by MTBs, and by a flotilla of five destroyers. Not a single torpedo or bomb found its target and the attackers lost seventeen aircraft to fighters and flak, including all six naval Swordfish, whose leader, Commander Esmonde, who had led the attacks on the Bismarck the previous year, was awarded a posthumous VC.

Arthur Aldridge of 217 Squadron flew during that afternoon's Beaufort attacks and came close to scoring a torpedo hit. Low cloud allowed him to get close to one of the big ships – he was never quite sure which one – and he dropped his torpedo in copybook fashion. His colleague Bill Carroll was

'Channel Dash': the formidable battleships *Scharnhorst* and *Gneisenau* steaming rapidly through the English Channel on 12 February 1942. (Photo: Crown Copyright)

flying in another Beaufort which also got its torpedo away, and then had to fly down the whole length of the *Gneisenau*, under fire, before getting back into cloud cover. Neither torpedo hit the target, but both men survived the day, and the war. However, several other 217 Squadron crews were less fortunate, and *'failed to return'* from their sorties against the big ships.

Aldridge was to write later of his Channel Dash experience that *chaos and confusion ruled*.[17] This view was shared by higher authority and the wider public, with the Times leader writer lamenting an event *mortifying to the pride of sea-power* and Churchill appointing a judicial Board of Enquiry to identify the causes of the failure.

The big German ships did not escape completely unscathed. Both the *Scharnhorst* and *Gneisenau* were damaged when they hit mines off the Dutch coast, and a Bomber Command raid later in February caused severe damage to the *Gneisenau*, which never again put to sea. The *Scharnhorst* did sail again and was sunk by British battleships in December 1943 at the Battle of the North Cape.

---

17   Aldridge & Ryan, *The Last Torpedo Flyers*, p.146.

3

The Response, 1943-45: Strike Wings

Key Decisions

The tide gradually began to turn for Coastal Command's anti-shipping campaign during 1942. The humiliation of the Channel Dash in February was a major catalyst for change, and one of the decisions taken after the Enquiry reported was that a new anti-shipping offensive should be planned and implemented by Coastal Command. The key decisions taken were to focus on attacking German ships with torpedoes, and to use the Bristol Beaufighter to make these strikes.

An important source of support for the escalation of attacks on German merchant shipping in the North Sea came from the Ministry of Economic Warfare (MEW). Analysis of intelligence reports in the first half of 1942 indicated that German merchant shipping capacity was becoming very stretched and that there was a shortage of experienced crews for the vessels that were available. This was the result of a combination of factors, including the diversion of merchant shipping capacity to supply the army in the Baltic, the conversion of merchantmen into flak ships, the effect of bombing raids on shipyards, which reduced the speed at which ships could be built and repaired, and the increasing reluctance of Swedish crews to sail in the North Sea.

Germany had responded to these problems by appointing senior Nazi Karl Kaufman as Reichskommissar for shipping, reporting directly to Hitler, with wide-ranging powers over all aspects of the shipping industry. As Gauleiter of Hamburg, Kaufman was well known in the German shipping industry, and he was tasked with building new merchant ships and making more effective use of the ships that were available. However, the MEW believed that the current German weakness could be exploited, and that successful attacks against the convoys sailing into Rotterdam could potentially have a significant impact on industrial production in the Ruhr.

Despite the high-level decisions taken in the first half of 1942, and the support of the MEW and the Admiralty, progress in implementing the new anti-shipping plans was slow. The realities of Britain's continuing resource constraints and the priority given to the strategic bombing offensive, as well as the struggles in the Mediterranean and Far East, meant that the original plans had to be scaled back, and Coastal Command continued to suffer from shortages of aircraft, crews and torpedoes. This was despite continual pressure from Air Chief Marshall Joubert, who in his dispatch expressed his frustration at the slowness of the Beaufighter's torpedo bombing acceptance trials, even advocating that these should be dispensed with. However, by late 1942 Coastal Command was ready and able to deploy its new anti-shipping force.

With Hindsight …

The British assessment of the shortage of German merchant shipping capacity in early 1942 was accurate, but the strategic significance of this was not properly recognised at the time by Britain's war leaders. The exceptionally cold winter of 1941-42 had exacerbated Germany's raw material supply problems, with the Baltic ports frozen closed for longer than usual and the alternative western route also affected by frozen seas and canals. A crucial German supply line therefore was vulnerable – iron ore was short and shipping was short; and the means to exploit this weakness had been identified and was under development – Strike Wings equipped with Beaufighters. However, the urgency was lacking at the top of the RAF to get these into action as quickly as possible. The strategic bombing campaign against Germany's industrial cities dominated British offensive thinking, from Churchill downwards, and other options were considered to be sideshows, rather than as real opportunities to strike a potentially decisive blow against the enemy.

After his appointment in May 1942, Kaufman worked quickly to restore the situation in the German merchant fleet, so that by the end of 1942 *the effect was to increase the lift of the German Mercantile Marine to an extent sufficient to offset, for the time being, the effects of our attacks.* The opportunity to hit the enemy hard when he was down had passed. Germany's merchant shipping fleet at the end of 1942 was back up to the full capacity required, *a system that was at the peak of its operational efficiency.*[1]

It therefore fell to the Strike Wings to drive this strong and determined enemy out of the of the North Sea after April 1943, rather than during the summer of 1942, when that enemy's supply line had been significantly more vulnerable.

New Tactics

A policy conference convened in May 1942 added substance to the outline plan that had been agreed for the new offensive. Importantly, this conference heard detailed feedback first-hand from experienced front-line squadron leaders and drew on operational experience gained in the Mediterranean

---

1   Joubert Dispatch, (TNA) AIR 15/773

theatre. A number of tactical principles were established for shipping strikes, which prevailed throughout the campaign until the end of the war.

First, if at all possible, attacks should be launched when the weather and light conditions were optimal. Low-level attacks against ships were most effective at dawn and dusk, and especially when there was some low cloud cover as well. Small German 'reporting vessels' off the Dutch coast and improved radar on shore meant that total surprise was increasingly difficult to achieve, so the attackers had to use every possible advantage.

Secondly, the strikes should be made in Wing strength and launched in two waves, with the initial wave using cannon fire to suppress the flak, allowing the second wave of torpedo bombers to achieve the ideal range, height and speed for launching their torpedoes. Typically, this would be at 800-1000 yards from the target, at a height of 100-200 feet, and with a speed of 200-250 knots. There should be as short a time as possible between the two waves of the attack, ideally no more than 20 seconds, giving the ships' defenders no time to recover from the first wave's barrage of cannon fire.

Thirdly, there should be a lot of fighter cover, ideally with two single seater fighters deployed for each attacking Beaufighter. This would not only keep losses low; it would also allow Beaufighters to concentrate on the ships, rather than worry about being bounced by enemy fighters.

These tactical decisions were documented and passed down to the front-line units to absorb and refine. Meanwhile the anti-shipping squadrons had begun to be re-equipped with Beaufighters, and some experienced crews were brought back from the Mediterranean.

New Aircraft and Weapons

Developed from the under-powered Beaufort, the Beaufighter Mark VIC, powered by twin 1,650 hp Bristol Hercules engines was the ideal aircraft for successful strikes on armed enemy convoys.

The Beaufighter had a crew of two: the pilot at the front, with a good field of vision; and a navigator/wireless operator around halfway back along the fuselage, with a clear Perspex cupola allowing all-round vision. As well as enabling the navigator to plot a course and keep a lookout against attack from above and behind, this view allowed him to observe and photograph the results of the strike. The crew were connected by intercom and communicated throughout the flight. Most crews formed a close-knit team, always flying together unless prevented by illness, injury or leave.

Earlier versions of the Beaufighter had proved their worth since their introduction into the RAF in 1940, mainly as a night-fighter. The future Dambuster leader Guy Gibson had enhanced his reputation in 1941 when he flew on a Beaufighter night-fighter squadron. The aircraft was rugged and agile, a well armoured machine that cruised at 200mph between sea level and 1,000ft (the Strike Wings' typical operating altitude) and it was capable of surviving much flak damage. Although vulnerable against a single seater fighter attack, it could dash away at a maximum speed of 350 mph if needed.

Bristol Beaufighter – fast, rugged, versatile and heavily-armed – the ideal aircraft for strikes against shipping. (Photo: Crown Copyright/ Vimpany archive)

Its routine operating range when armed was around 1,000 miles, sufficient to roam the North Sea, the Channel and the Bay of Biscay.

Two variants were developed for the two distinct anti-shipping roles. For the initial attack, the 'flak suppression' variant was equipped with four powerful Hispano-Suiza 20mm cannon, mounted within the fuselage beneath the pilot and firing through the nose. It had in addition six Browning .303 machine guns, four in the port wing and two in the starboard. Mounted in the navigator's cupola, to fire backwards and defend against an attack from the rear, was a .303 Vickers K or Browning machine gun. The flak suppression Beaufighters could also deliver two 250 lb bombs, one slung under each wing, but after the first few Wing strikes the aircraft were rarely armed with these.

The torpedo strike variant, known as the 'Torbeau', was equipped to carry and launch a torpedo. It too was armed with four cannon and the navigator's machine gun, but with no wing-mounted machine guns. In 1942 a new strengthened torpedo, the Mark XV, with an 18' diameter, was developed specifically for aircraft use, designed to enter the water at higher speed and with a more controlled trajectory.

236 (Anti-flak) and 254 (Torbeau) Squadrons took delivery of their Mark VIC Beaufighters over the summer of 1942 and in November formed the North Coates Strike Wing, part of Coastal Command's 16 Group. In January 1943 they were joined by 143 (Anti-flak) Squadron equipped with the Beaufighter Mark IIF, similar to the VIC but with even more powerful 1,772 hp Hercules engines. The Beaufighter Wing was an integrated force, sharing a base, training together and with specific roles to play in coordinated strikes at Wing strength, directed in the air by a nominated wing leader, usually an experienced torpedo bomber pilot.

From the late spring of 1943 onwards, 236 and 143 Squadrons could carry even more firepower, now able also to be armed with eight rocket projectiles

Armed Torbeau and crew – a wartime publicity photograph! (Photo: Crown Copyright/Vimpany archive)

(RP) fired from two racks of four rails, one rack suspended beneath each wing. The effectiveness of the initial high-explosive 60 lb rockets proved disappointing, but a new armour-piercing 25 lb projectile introduced towards the end of 1943 was much more successful. This weapon was less difficult to aim, and by striking just below the waterline it was capable of sinking vessels, not just damaging the superstructure. It was particularly useful against ships in shallow water, where torpedoes could not be used.

Crew Training

Crews joined the Strike Wing squadrons from the specialist Operations Training Unit (OTU) at RAF Catfoss in Yorkshire, where pilots and navigators, some experienced and converting to the Beaufighter and others with no operational experience, would spend several weeks training for combat. Torbeau crews also trained for torpedo bombing at the RAF's Torpedo Training Unit (TTU), based first at Castle Kennedy and then at Turnberry, both on the south-west coast of Scotland.

Accidents and fatalities during training were common. At the OTU, trainee navigator Dick Vimpany was first crewed up with Canadian pilot Carl

A fearsome anti-ship weapon – a Beaufighter of 236 Squadron armed with eight Rocket Projectiles. (Photo: Crown Copyright/Air Historical Branch)

Caldwell, who was killed shortly afterwards in a flying accident. Vimpany then flew with Squadron Leader Freddie Gardiner, an experienced pilot who had flown Spitfires during the Battle of Britain and been shot down and wounded, and was now returning to operations after a tour training glider pilots. They completed the torpedo training course and joined 254 Squadron at the end of April 1943. They flew together in action for the next twelve months.

Tough Targets

Until the arrival of the Beaufighter, strikes against enemy shipping had typically involved a small group of aircraft, or even a single aircraft, attempting to find and sink merchant vessels. Through the course of 1942 the new tactics described earlier had been developed, based around larger-scale attacks on the increasingly large and well-defended enemy convoys.

By 1943 German merchant convoys typically comprised several armed merchant ships of between 1,000-10,000 tons, carrying high-grade iron ore, coal, oil or other strategic war material. As well as German merchantmen, many convoys included ships requisitioned from occupied countries such as Norway and the Netherlands, and Swedish ships sailing under contract. At the start of 1943 it was estimated that 40% of iron ore supplied into Rotterdam was still being carried by Swedish ships, which then took coal and coke back to Sweden.

The target – an enemy convoy, the ships flying anti-aircraft balloons; photographed by a reconnaissance aircraft on May 17 1943, this convoy was attacked successfully – one merchant ship was sunk and all aircraft returned safely. (Photo: Crown copyright/AIR 28/595)

The merchant ships were protected by armed escort vessels of the German Navy (*Kriegsmarine*), usually with a ratio of around three escorts to each merchant ship. Well trained German naval gunners also manned guns on the merchantmen themselves. Typical escort vessels were M-Class minesweepers, heavily armed, usually with five large calibre guns, including 105mm. Smaller escorts were converted trawlers of around 500 tons, armed with six to eight cannon of different calibres, including at least one of 88mm, as well as 37mm and 20mm, and several 7.62mm machine guns.[2] Most formidable and feared were the larger, dedicated flak-ships known as *Sperrbrecher* or 'barrier-breakers'. These were former merchant ships of up to 8,000 tons, their hulls strengthened to make them harder to sink, and packed with flak defences.

Together, these armed ships could put up an intense wall of flak through which their attackers had to fly to engage the merchant ships. Their heavy guns were capable of firing at 15 rounds per minute, the shells bursting in the air around the aircraft. The lighter 20mm weapons could achieve firing rates of over 200 rounds per minute, including tracer to assist aiming, and were highly dangerous to aircraft flying at low altitude.

Further defensive measures included barrage balloons tethered to vessels by steel cables, lethal to any aircraft that struck one and difficult to fly around in the heat of a fast, low-level attack. At one stage the Germans experimented

---

2   Nesbit, *The Strike Wings*, p.26.

TO FORCE THE ENEMY OFF THE SEA'

with defensive flame throwers, although these were not effective, and disliked by the ships' crews. Convoys would sail with the merchantmen in line astern, led by minesweepers and with other escort vessels positioned on both beams and at the rear. Depending on the location of the strike, further threats to attacking aircraft could include flak from land-based gun batteries, especially around German-held ports, and escorting or responding Luftwaffe fighters, including single-seater Messerschmidt Me109s or Focke-Wolf FW190s.

A 'Wing Strike' operation

The primary objective of a strike was to sink the merchant ships and their cargo, while minimising the loss of attacking aircraft. After a detailed operational briefing, based on weather, intelligence and reconnaissance reports, the Strike Wing would take off and form up over its base, proceed to a rendezvous with its fighter escort, and then head out across the sea to seek out the targeted convoy.

To achieve surprise, the Wing flew at low level and in radio silence, if possible taking advantage of weather conditions such as cloud or poor visibility. At the point of interception with the convoy the anti-flak Beaufighters in the formation, as many as 24 aircraft, would climb with the wing leader to around 3,000 feet. They would then tighten into close

The Wing's Beaufighters forming up over North Coates airfield before a Strike, never an easy manoeuvre. (Photo: Crown Copyright/Vimpany archive)

formation for a diving attack on the convoy, usually in groups of three, each of these having a specific ship at which they had been briefed to aim their cannon and rocket fire. The diving Beaufighters concentrated their fire on the escorts, seeking to destroy the guns or drive the gunners away from their posts. Sometimes a number of the Beaufighters in the diving anti-flak attack would also release 250 lb bombs, although early in the campaign these were replaced by rocket projectiles.

Following immediately behind the anti-flak Beaufighters were the Torbeaus, usually between eight and twelve in number. Flying in pairs, these aircraft would stay at low level, typically 150-250 feet, and make their run immediately after the first wave anti-flak attack, which had hopefully suppressed the defensive fire from the ships. The Torbeaus would fly towards their pre-selected merchant ships, 'jinxing' in level flight before straightening up and releasing their torpedo, then opening fire with their cannon as they flew at high speed over the ship they had targeted.

The greatest impact was achieved if the attack was executed as a single pass, with the Torbeaus following closely behind the anti-flak attack before the ships' gunners had recovered from the initial cannon and rocket onslaught. A larger number of torpedoes in the water gave the ships less chance of avoiding them. If not brought down during their run, the Torbeaus would immediately break for home, leaving the anti-flak aircraft to consider any further attacks on the ships. The escorting fighters, usually Spitfires or Mustangs, would engage any enemy fighters which appeared at any point in the operation, preventing these from getting at the Beaufighters.

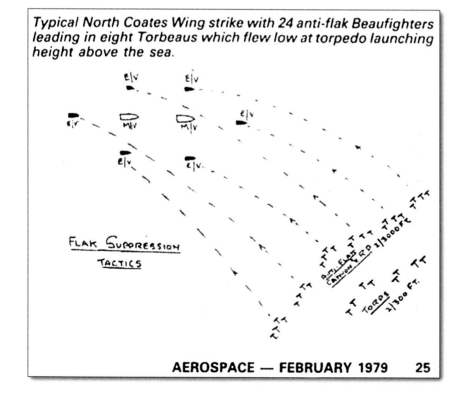

Typical North Coates Wing strike with 24 anti-flak Beaufighters leading in eight Torbeaus which flew low at torpedo launching height above the sea.

FLAK SUPPRESSION
TACTICS

AEROSPACE — FEBRUARY 1979   25

254 Squadron CO Paddy Burns' hand-drawn diagram illustrating Strike Wing tactics. (Photo: Aerospace magazine, with permission)

'Strike': an image capturing the speed and intensity of a Beaufighter attack on an enemy ship. (Photo: Crown Copyright/Air Historical Branch)

This typical Wing Strike was illustrated thirty-five years later by Paddy Burns, CO of 254 Squadron during 1944, in a lecture to the Royal Aerospace Society's Historical Group and reproduced in an article in Aerospace magazine.[3]

A wing strike was a fast and furious battle fought at close quarters between the attacking aircrew and the defending naval gunners, both adversaries brave and resolute. The action might be over in just four minutes, leaving ships sinking, damaged or on fire, and with any Beaufighters that were hit either exploding, crashing into the waves or limping away damaged. Film footage of wing strikes, taken with gun-mounted cameras, captures the speed of the encounters and the wall of fire faced, as well as the devastating effect of the cannon and rocket fire aimed at the ships.

Back at base, usually less than three hours after taking off, the crews were debriefed, films were taken for developing and analysis, and an overall picture would emerge of the results of the strike, identifying which ships were sunk or damaged, and any aircraft and crews that were lost.

---

3   Group Captain R.E. Burns, 'Anti-Shipping Strikes 1939-45', *Aerospace Magazine*, February 1979.

The first strike – hard lessons learned

The new North Coates Strike Wing launched its first strike on 20 November 1942. At this stage, the Wing consisted of 236 Squadron with anti-flak Beaufighters, each of which also carried two 250lb bombs, and 254 Squadron in Torbeaus. The Torbeau crews had arrived at North Coates just two weeks earlier, after a period of torpedo bombing training at several different locations around the country. The Wing had flown together on practice strikes only twice, on the two days before this first operational strike, with 236 Squadron having spent much of the previous two months flying in twos and threes on reconnaissance and search-and-rescue missions.

Twenty-five Beaufighters, comprising sixteen anti-flak aircraft and nine Torbeaus, took off at 1500 hours and headed to Coltishall in Norfolk, 90 miles away, to rendezvous with an escorting squadron of Spitfires that were based there. The target was a convoy sailing off the Hook of Holland, consisting of a single large merchant vessel being towed by a tug, and six escorts. By chance, a further three German anti-flak ships on a separate mission were approaching the convoy from the south, which meant that the Strike Wing would be exposed to fire from nine flak ships in all.

The fighters did not appear at the rendezvous on schedule, so the Wing leader decided to head for the convoy without them, to intercept the target before it could reach the shelter of the shore batteries on the Hook of Holland. One group of four anti-flak aircraft missed the signal to turn east towards the convoy, and another aircraft had to turn back with engine trouble, so that the force arriving over the German ships was made up of only eleven anti-flak aircraft and the nine Torbeaus, and no fighters.

The attack was launched in accordance with the agreed tactics, with the anti-flak aircraft climbing then executing a diving attack against the escort ships, while the Torbeaus got into position to attack the merchant ship, approaching from the direction of the Dutch coast. Despite the wall of flak put up by the ships, eight of the Torbeaus got their torpedoes away. However, at least three of these hit the seabed before they reached the ships, and no hits were observed by any of the others. The concentrated flak from the convoy scored multiple hits on the attacking aircraft, whilst out of range of the anti-aircraft fire the Wing was attacked by four single-seat FW190 fighters.

The balance sheet for the Strike did not make good reading. Three Beaufighters had been lost and their crews killed, including the Wing Commander and one of 236 Squadron's flight commanders. (The airmen killed were: W/Cdr. Fraser, P/O Griffin, S/Ldr. Edney, F/Sgt. Haddow, P/O Sargent. F/Sgt. Heskel).

Two more aircraft had been written off when crash landing back in Britain and a further five had suffered serious damage. In return, the tug had been sunk and two of the escorts damaged, with some loss of life, but the primary target, later identified as a Kriegsmarine 'experimental' ship, the *Coburg*, had come through the strike almost unscathed.

A combination of operational failures and bad luck had turned the strike into a costly failure. Pressing on without the Spitfires, which had taken off but failed to link up with the Beaufighters, exposed the Wing to the German fighters. The size of the convoy escort, reinforced by the separate group of ships sailing nearby, was greater than expected and presented a major challenge to a Wing that had been reduced to only eleven anti-flak aircraft. There were too few aircraft to suppress so much flak. The Torbeau attack took place from a position which meant the torpedoes were launched into shallow water and hit the seabed.

The Coastal Command Review accorded only two short paragraphs to this first Wing Strike, citing as mitigating factors that the Wing had attacked a different convoy from the one intended, and that poor weather had also been a factor. However, the scale of the failure and the losses, after such high hopes for the new aircraft and new tactics, caused a drop in Wing morale, and the aircrews feared a return to the bad old days of 'forlorn hope' missions.

After the unlucky, but costly, outcome of this first strike, Air Chief Marshall Joubert, still the Air Officer Commanding Coastal Command, realised that '*only by hard and meticulous training could the force be welded into an efficient fighting weapon*'.[4] He therefore withdrew the Wing from the line and appointed a new Wing Leader to work the unit up into the state of efficiency required to take on the German convoys successfully.

New leadership – ready to strike again

The replacement Wing Leader, and new Commanding Officer of 236 Squadron, was twenty-six-year-old Wing Commander Neil Wheeler DFC. Originally a bomber pilot, he had previously spent several years developing and leading one of the RAF's photo reconnaissance units, flying Spitfires, and was a pioneer of the effective but highly dangerous low-level reconnaissance mission.

'Nebby' Wheeler was an outstanding leader, who would go on to have a glittering RAF career. With his operational experience and tactical acumen, he quickly recognised the inherent potential of the Strike Wing concept, the suitability of the Beaufighter as a 'ship buster', and the courage and skill of his aircrews. He took immediate steps to review and refine the Wing's tactics and initiated a rigorous training programme.

Wheeler articulated clearly the conditions necessary for a successful wing strike:[5]

- Prior reconnaissance and accurate intelligence, to identify suitable target convoys.
- The anti-flak sections must protect the Torbeaus and create a clear field of fire for these to launch their torpedoes; ideally this was to be achieved by groups of three anti-flak Beaufighters simultaneously attacking each escort vessel and suppressing its fire.
- The Torbeaus should operate in 'fluid pairs' with each pair having a pre-selected target merchant vessel; torpedoes should only be dropped into

---

4   Joubert dispatch, (TNA) AIR 15/773.
5   Nesbit, *The Strike Wings*, p. 41.

waters where there was sufficient depth, at least 50 feet, to avoid uselessly striking the shallow seabed or sandbanks off the Dutch Coast.

- Most importantly, no Strike would be carried out without the protection of single-seat fighter escorts. By 1943 more fighters were becoming available from bases in East Anglia with the range and duration to successfully confront the Me109s and FW190s based along the Dutch Coast.

Wheeler was an inspired choice as leader of the North Coates Strike Wing and instrumental in the success it enjoyed for the rest of the war. Following the addition of 143 Squadron to the Wing and the introduction of some new crews from the Beaufighter OTU and Torpedo Training Units into 236 and 254 Squadrons, a period of the intensive training was initiated. This included detachments to the torpedo training establishments, where numerous convoy attack exercises were held, dropping dummy torpedoes. In early 1943 the mood in the North Coates Strike Wing was positive again, and the highly trained Wing was ready for action again.

4

North Coates Strike Wing Operations

The North Sea and its weather make for an unforgiving theatre of war. Stand today on the airfield at North Coates and look out from the bleak shoreline, across the sea. In bad weather it is dark and sinister, and even when the sun is shining it feels dangerous. Whether flying into the intense sound and fury of a Wing Strike, or on a lonely solo reconnaissance mission along the Dutch coast at dawn, the young airmen from North Coates rarely betrayed how they felt, even to their closest comrades. They were a close-knit group of young men, doing their duty and doing their job. Many aircrews *failed to return*, falling prey to flak or enemy fighters or an unknown mishap. Today one can only try to imagine what fear and trepidation a young airman would have felt when taking off and, if his luck held, his relief on returning safely.

The North Coates Wing covered the 'Hook-to-Elbe' sector of the North Sea, from the exit of the Kiel Canal in the north down to the turn into the Rotterdam port complex in the south.

Overview

This chapter chronicles some of the most important Strikes and other operations carried out by the North Coates Wing after April 1943. Although mainly chronological, it is not a comprehensive day-to-day operational diary; it is a narrative that traces the development of the two-year campaign and highlights the increasing success that the Wing achieved. Formed in November 1942, the Wing initially comprised 236 and 254 Squadrons, with 143 Squadron joining in January 1943, from which time the Wing could deploy over thirty aircraft. In October 1944, 143 Squadron left North Coates to join one of the Strike Wings based in Scotland, but 254 and 236 Squadrons remained together until the end of the war in Europe in May 1945.

The descriptions of the actions covered are based mainly on the squadrons' Operations Record Books (ORBs) and supported by other, secondary sources, in particular Nesbit, who drew heavily on the recollections of many of the aircrew who participated in the Strikes. A primary source of particular

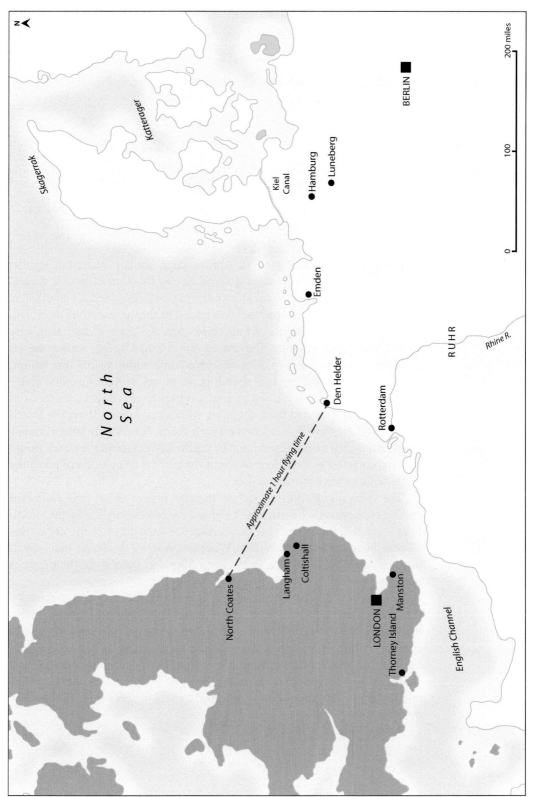

The North Coates Strike Wing main area of operations, 1943-45; squadrons could be detached as required to Kent, Cornwall, or Scotland.

focus is Dick Vimpany's logbook, and the notes he made in his copies of the various books published about the campaign, which are his personal recollections of some of the Strikes and other operations that he took part in.

18 April 1943: First success

Wing Strike off Texel

Attacking force		Operating conditions	
Torbeaus:	9 from 254 Sqn	Take-off time:	13:20
Anti-Flak:	6 from 236 Sqn	Flight Duration:	2 hours 15 minutes
	6 from 143 Sqn	Cloud:	At 10,000 ft
Commanded by:	W/Cdr. Wheeler	Visibility:	4-6 miles
Escort:	38 fighters in total	Wind:	10-20 mph

Early on the morning of 18 April a large convoy had been sighted heading north from the Hook of Holland, having left Rotterdam at first light. It consisted of eight merchant ships carrying coal (destined for Sweden as part payment for the iron ore that was traded in the opposite direction) and was sailing in two columns of four ships each. All the merchantman were flying anti-aircraft balloons. The convoy was escorted by four minesweepers and four specialist flak ships, armed with a combination of 105mm, 88mm, 35mm and 20mm calibre anti-aircraft guns, as well as light machine guns.[1] Each merchant column was led by a minesweeper, reflecting the threat from mines that the RAF had been dropping with some success along the Dutch coast, and there were three escorts on each beam. This heavily armed convoy clearly presented a tough opponent for the Strike Wing, and the attack would be a rigorous test of the effectiveness of the tactical changes made since the costly failure of five months earlier.

The Wing successfully picked up its large fighter escort over Coltishall and set out across the North Sea. It sighted the convoy slightly further north than expected, but otherwise the intelligence used to brief the crews was all absolutely correct, and W/Cdr. Wheeler launched the Strike precisely as planned, drawing on all the tactical planning and training of the previous months.

The twelve anti-flak Beaufighters climbed to 1,500 feet and executed a devastating diving attack with cannon and light bombs, causing severe damage to several escorts and significantly reducing the intensity of fire coming up from the German ships. Before the ships' gunners could recover, the Torbeaus made their run, coming in around 175 feet above sea level and dropping their torpedoes at around 1,000 yards from the merchant ship they had targeted. They followed through their attack with cannon as they flew over the ships.

---

1   Nesbit, *The Strike Wings*, p.45

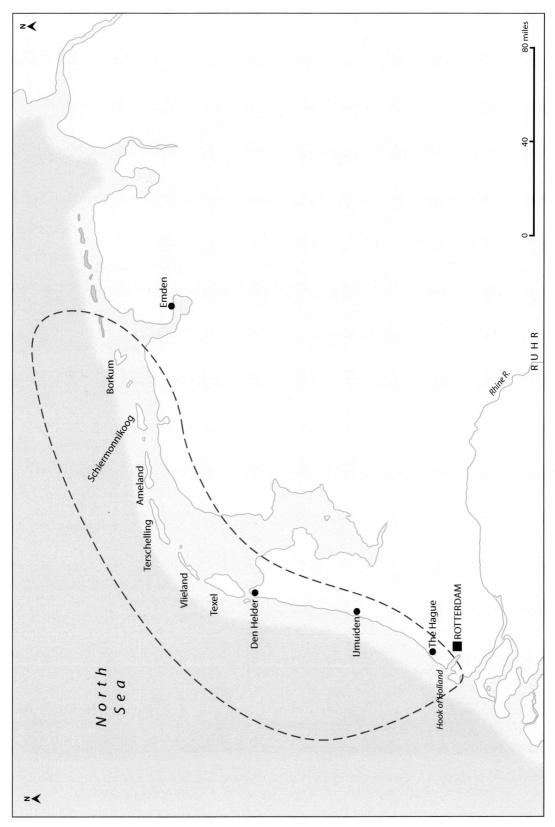

The 'Battlefield': Between 1942 and 1945 almost 100 Beaufighters were lost in the area indicated above; almost all of the aircrews lost their lives.

Anti-flak Beaufighter attacking a minesweeper escort with cannon (top), then flying past the ship at more than 200 miles per hour (bottom), off Texel on 18 April 1943. (Photos: Crown Copyright/AIR 28/595 and Air Historical Branch)

With so many torpedoes in the water at the same time, the target had little hope of taking avoiding action, and at least three torpedoes hit the largest ship in the convoy. The ORB records that *Large explosions were seen and columns of smoke and debris seen rising to a height of 100 feet.* This ship was the 4,903 ton *Hoegh Carrier*, which sank almost immediately. A number of escorts were damaged, two of them so severely that they had to leave the convoy and head for the nearest port.

The entire Strike lasted only four minutes before the Wing formed up and headed for home. Two of the attacking aircraft were slightly damaged, but otherwise the Wing returned unscathed to North Coates, where they received an enthusiastic welcome from the ground personnel.

This first Wing Strike had been a complete success, a well-planned and well executed precision attack, sinking a major target for no loss. It fully vindicated the strategic and tactical decisions made over the previous twelve months. The only disappointment expressed was by the RAF fighter pilots, who regretted that the Germans had not sent up their fighters to provide some opposition.

29 April 1943: Even better encore

Wing Strike off Vlieland

Attacking force		Operating conditions	
Torbeaus:	12 from 254 Sqn	Take-off time:	16:40
Anti-Flak:	9 from 236 Sqn	Flight Duration:	2 hours 30 minutes
	6 from 143 Sqn	Cloud:	Light, 2-3,000 feet
Commanded by:	W/Cdr. Wheeler	Visibility:	2-3 miles
Escort:	24 Spitfires + 6 Mustangs	Wind:	Light

Less than two weeks after the first successful strike, an RAF fighter patrol reported another large convoy seen heading north from Rotterdam. A reconnaissance by a Beaufighter from 143 Squadron confirmed the convoy's position, and further details were obtained from photographs taken by a Mustang sent out for this purpose. The convoy consisted of six merchant ships, all flying balloons, and nine escorts. This was clearly a valuable target, and a Strike was launched in the late afternoon.

The rendezvous with the fighter escorts out of Coltishall was successful and the attacking force set out over the North Sea, made up of fifty-seven aircraft in total. It caught the convoy ten miles off the island of Vlieland. This convoy too was formed of two columns, surrounded by the escort minesweepers and anti-flak ships, and the Torbeaus split into groups to launch their attack.

The diving attack by the anti-flak Beaufighters beat down the fire from the German gunners and the Torbeaus launched their attacks against the port column of merchantmen, at 1804 hours precisely. The first Torbeau group targeted the leading merchant ship, launching five torpedoes at a height of 120 feet. (The torpedo in the sixth aircraft 'hung up'). The second

Four North Coates Beaufighters completing their low pass over an escort and a merchant ship, avoiding the balloon cable, on the Strike off Vlieland on 29 April 1943. (Photo: Crown Copyright/AIR 28/595)

group attacked the next merchant ship in the column, at the same height, and all torpedoes were dropped. Most Torbeaus opened fire with their cannon after launching their torpedo, seeking to cause further damage as well as to deter the German gunners as they flew over the ships.

On this occasion the results observed by the crew at the time corresponded to later intelligence reports. Torpedo hits were observed on the two leading merchantmen in the port column and on one of the minesweepers on the starboard side of the convoy. All three of these ships were sunk. The merchantmen were the Swedish *Narvik*, of 4,251 tons, and the Dutch *Alundra*, of 4,930 tons. At least four other escort vessels suffered significant damage.

Various aircraft reported being engaged by German twin-engine fighters, either Ju88 or ME 110, but no damage was sustained by the Beaufighters, and just over an hour after the Strike the Wing landed back at North Coates. This Strike was not without loss, however, and during the attack a Beaufighter from 143 Squadron was seen to *spin in from around 100 feet* with the crew killed instantly (F/O Wilsden, Sgt. Thompson).

In under two weeks the Germans had lost three large merchant ships, around 14,000 tons in total, and one minesweeper, for the loss of one aircraft. In addition, six naval escorts had been severely damaged. These were impressive results, vindicating the creation of the Strike Wing and the tactics it had developed.

1 May 1943: An unfortunate diversion: chasing the cruiser *Nurnburg*

German capital ships remained a threat in 1943, particularly in northern waters, menacing the Arctic convoys on their way to the Russian port of Murmansk, and attacking these warships remained a high priority for the Royal Navy and for Coastal Command. On 1 May intelligence was received that the German cruiser *Nurnberg*, accompanied by three destroyers, was moving along the south-west coast of Norway and the North Coates Wing, comprising thirty-one aircraft led by S/Ldr. Denholm of 236 Squadron, was tasked to seek out and attack these ships. The force was deployed with 236 Squadron in the van, the Torbeaus of 254 Squadron in the centre, and 143 Squadron providing the rear-guard.

This mission took the Wing well beyond the range of fighter cover but within the range of the German fighter squadrons based in southern Norway. The Wing could not find the *Nurnberg* but were themselves found by the German Me109s and FW190s, which attacked the middle and rear of the British formation. In a desperate action, the Torbeaus had to jettison their torpedoes and every aircraft had to scramble to try to escape from the faster, more manoeuvrable single-seat fighters.

The Germans succeeded in shooting down three Torbeaus and two Beaufighters from 143 Squadron, with only twenty-six aircraft escaping to Wick in northern Scotland, four hours after taking off. S/Ldr. Denholm reported that the losses would have been very much higher but for the determined defence put up by 143 Squadron acting as rear-guard. S/Ldr. Ritchie, who led 143 Squadron on the mission, was awarded an immediate DFC and F/Sgt. Ceybird, who returned safely but whose navigator (F/Sgt. Baker) was killed, was awarded an immediate DFM. (The other airmen lost were F/Sgt. Foster, Sgt. Curnuck, S/Ldr. Pett, F/Sgt. Crossley, F/Sgt. Poore, F/Sgt. Jones, Sgt. Marshall, Sgt. Highstead).

This unfortunate sortie, with the Wing losing nine airmen only days after delivering two successful Strikes for the loss of only one crew, reinforced Wheeler's determination not to mount Wing Strikes without a sufficient fighter escort

17 May 1943: Back in business

Wing Strike off Texel

Attacking force		Operating conditions	
Torbeaus:	11 from 254 Sqn	Take-off time:	15:15
Anti-Flak:	9 from 236 Sqn	Flight Duration:	2 hours 20 minutes
	6 from 143 Sqn	Cloud:	Little or no cloud
Commanded by:	W/Cdr. Wheeler	Visibility:	5-10 miles
Escort:	c.60 Spitfires	Wind:	Light, variable

This was the first Strike flown by S/Ldr. Freddie Gardiner and Sgt. Dick Vimpany, in Torbeau 'H'. Also flying on this Strike was an old school friend of Dick's, Sgt. Freddy Hinks, the regular navigator for pilot Tom Cochrane, in Torbeau 'Q', this crew having joined the squadron several months earlier.

The enemy convoy was intercepted and attacked off the island of Texel, around an hour's flying time from the Wing's North Coates base. It comprised several merchant ships, sailing in two columns, protected by minesweepers. The anti-flak aircraft dived on the escorts in the now standard pattern of attack, with 236 Squadron using bombs as well as cannon. The Torbeaus divided into three groups for the Strike, two of these launching their torpedoes at the starboard column and other one at the port column.

Gardiner and Vimpany's Torbeau was one of the aircraft that attacked the leading merchant ship in the port column. No hits were seen but Dick Vimpany reported seeing a column of white smoke or steam rising from the target. This was also observed by the aircraft in one of the groups that had attacked the starboard column.

The combined observations of all the attacking Torbeaus suggested that two merchant ships and at least two escorts had probably been hit by torpedoes, and several others damaged by cannon shells and set on fire. The escorting Spitfires reported that the largest merchant ship (which they estimated at 8,000 tons) and two of the escorting minesweepers had been left sinking after the Strike. The merchant ship sunk was later identified as the 2,964-ton *Kyphissia* and it was confirmed that a minesweeper and an anti-flak ship had also been destroyed. No aircraft were lost in the encounter.

The observations reported by the crews and recorded in the squadron ORBs reflect the fast and furious nature of a Wing Strike. Pilots were throwing their aircraft around the sky at over 200 mph, to try to avoid the wall of flak streaming up from the convoy, as well as the other aircraft attacking the same ship. This was all accompanied by a cacophony of noise coming from the engines, cannon fire, and shells bursting all around. It was not easy therefore, for the crews to see everything that was happening and then report it at the debriefing. On this occasion only one torpedo hit had been observed, but it was clear that there had been at least two others, and probably more.

This appears to have been a copy-book Strike carried out in ideal conditions, with three ships sunk for no loss to the Wing. Indeed, most of Wheeler's 'conditions for success' applied on this day: good prior knowledge of the target's location; a lot of fighter cover – more than two Spitfires to every Beaufighter, deterring the German fighters from appearing on this occasion; and good coordination of the anti-flak and torpedo bombing attacks. The Torbeaus also selected their targets carefully and attacked these in groups, releasing several torpedoes into the water at the same time and increasing the likelihood of a hit.

The ORB Summary concluded that *All aircraft returned safely.* In his logbook Dick Vimpany simply recorded: '*Strike. Texel.*' For him, this first 'business trip' had been a good one.

A Strike launched on 24 May did not succeed in sinking any vessels. Gardiner and Vimpany flew on that mission, again in Torbeau 'H', launching their torpedo from a height of 100 feet, at 800-1,000 yards distance from the convoy. However, the weather was poor, with low cloud and rain, and no hits were observed. A number of Beaufighters suffered damage from flak, but all returned safely.

254 Squadron Torbeaus 'jinxing' on their run in towards the merchant ships, on the strike of 17 May 1943 off Texel.
(Photo: Crown Copyright/AIR 28/595)

Looking back to observe the damaged merchant vessel – and the balloon whose cable had been avoided, off Texel on 17 May 1943.
(Photo: Crown Copyright/AIR 28/595)

Three Beaufighters attack an escort with cannon fire on the unsuccessful Strike of 24 May 1943. (Photo: Crown Copyright/AIR 28/595)

13 June 1943: The intensity increases

Wing Strike off Den Helder

Attacking force		Operating conditions	
Torbeaus:	11 from 254 Sqn	Take-off time:	20:44
Anti-Flak:	9 from 236 Sqn	Flight Duration:	2 hours 16 minutes
	9 from 143 Sqn	Cloud:	2-3,000 feet
Commanded by:	W/Cdr. Wheeler	Visibility:	10-15 miles
Escort:	c.50 Spitfires	Wind:	10 mph

The next Strike was launched on 13 June (although Gardiner and Vimpany did not fly on this mission). In the interim the Wing had received a visit from the King and Queen, and then also the Air Minister, so morale was high even though it had been nearly a month since the Wing's last successful Strike.

The German convoy was sighted off Den Helder, the main naval port on the Dutch coast and heavily defended by shore batteries. It consisted of three merchant ships, the largest of which was the *Stadt Emden*, of 5,180 tons, which had also been part of the convoy that had been targeted unsuccessfully on 24 May. The escort was large, comprising four flak ships and five minesweepers. This high ratio of escorts to merchantmen reflected the success of the Strikes over the previous two months, as the Germans sought to counter the RAF's successful new anti-shipping tactics.

This Strike was a fierce engagement, with each side at full strength and the escorts putting up a tremendous curtain of flak. Ten Torbeaus attacked in their usual fluid pairs and seven successfully released their torpedoes, aiming at the *Stadt Emden*. The concentration of so many Torbeaus on the main target resulted in three aircraft not getting their torpedoes away, due to being *outsighted by others going in to attack*. A torpedo hit was seen on the *Stadt Emden* and explosions were observed on two other ships, and at least four minesweepers were left damaged and on fire. The *Stadt Emden* and one flak ship were later confirmed as sunk and four other escorts badly damaged. One aircraft of 143 Squadron was shot down and its crew killed. This was S/Ldr. Ritchie who had won the DFC for engaging the enemy fighters during the desperate action on

Beaufighter on the Strike of 13 June off Den Helder, at wave height and barely visible against the sea, attacking an escort obscured by the smoke caused by cannon shells striking. (Photo: Crown Copyright/AIR 28/595)

1 May, and his navigator, F/O Marsden. One 254 Squadron Torbeau pilot was wounded by shrapnel but managed to return safely to base. The 236 Squadron ORB notes that the fighter cover was provided by four squadrons of Spitfires and that on this occasion, perhaps understandably *no enemy aircraft were sufficiently imprudent to appear.*

The ORB accounts of this Strike mentions another hazard for crews. The radio equipment in one Torbeau caught fire, and the crew had to return to base – although not before putting the fire out with the help of a tin of orange juice! This Strike was also notable for being the first to be reported on by the BBC, with Richard Dimbleby interviewing W/Cdr. Neil Wheeler for the One O'Clock News, with the sound of Beaufighters taking off in the background. Another successful Strike, coming shortly after a Royal visit, and now some public recognition for the Wing, ensured that morale was indeed high at North Coates.

22 June 1943: New weapons, but not successful

Wing Strike off The Hague

Attacking force		Operating conditions	
Torbeaus:	12 from 254 Sqn	Take-off time:	15:42
Anti-Flak:	10 from 236 Sqn	Flight Duration:	2 hrs 30 mins
	12 from 143 Sqn	Cloud:	Low, in small amounts
Commanded by:	W/Cdr. Wheeler	Visibility:	4-5 miles
Escort:	c.50 Spitfires & Typhoons	Wind:	Light

Early in the morning of 22 June, two aircraft from 254 Squadron on separate reconnaissance patrols both sighted a large convoy heading south towards the Hook of Holland (the entrance to the channel into Rotterdam). The convoy consisted of five Swedish merchantmen and twelve escort vessels. As had become customary, the merchant ships were sailing in two columns, with the escorting minesweepers ahead of each column, and the flak ships all along both beams. The convoy was moving at around 6 knots and some of the merchant ships were flying anti-aircraft balloons.

Although the convoy was spotted early in the morning, it was not until late afternoon that a fighter escort became available, with three squadrons of Spitfires making their rendezvous with the Wing over Coltishall. Two squadrons of Typhoons were to cover the Wing's return from the strike. The Strike Wing was at full strength, deploying 34 aircraft and equipped for the first time with rockets, with each of the anti-flak Beaufighters carrying eight high-explosive 60 lb projectiles, in addition to their cannon.

This large force arrived over the convoy shortly after 17:00 hours. Although a measure of surprise was achieved, the delay had allowed the Germans to reinforce the escort with an additional three flak ships, making this convoy the most heavily defended that the Wing had so far attacked. It was probably not the ideal target on which to test out new weapons and make the tactical changes required to accommodate these.

Beaufighter crashing into the sea during the strike of 22 June 1943 off the Hague; photographed by Dick Vimpany. (Photo: Crown Copyright/Vimpany archive)

This attack went in from the seaward side of the convoy, coming out of the afternoon sun. The twenty-two anti-flak aircraft fired their one hundred and seventy-six rockets at the surprised and stunned convey escorts, who

were under rocket fire for the first time. However, instead of following in immediately, as they would have done after a cannon attack, the Torbeaus were held back momentarily in order to avoid the danger of being hit by the rockets. This pause gave the ships' gunners more time to recover, and the Torbeaus were exposed to intensive, accurate, light flak as they made their torpedo runs at four of the merchant vessels. The slight delay also allowed these ships to take what the ORB described as *violent evasive action*, turning towards the Torbeaus. The overall result was that although all of the Torbeaus got their torpedoes away successfully, no hits were observed and two Torbeaus were shot down, seen on fire and crashing in the sea. Dick Vimpany photographed one of these crashes, with the dinghy released by the impact with the sea visible in the photo. Several more Torbeaus were badly damaged, one of these by a balloon cable as well as flak.

The overall impression on the day was that the rockets had succeeded in damaging some escort vessels, leaving them on fire. However, Dick Vimpany, commenting on the photographs that he and others took, suggested that '*all the rockets missed*' and his account of the attack later refers to the rockets being used for the first time '*not too successfully*'. German records revealed after the war that three flak ships had in fact been hit by rockets, but the damage was minor and limited to their superstructures. The merchant ships suffered only minor damage from cannon fire.

The Germans too introduced new weapons during this battle. One of these was a flame thrower, which looked fearsome but was not effective against an aircraft flying at over 200 miles per hour, although it was potentially distracting for its crew.[2] The other was a rocket that contained a parachute with a 100-metre trailing cable. This was designed to be launched into the path of an attacking Torbeau, aiming for the cable to unfold and snag the aircraft as it flew overhead. It did not damage any Beaufighters during this attack, but did have some success later in the war, when explosive charges were also fitted to the parachute.

This Strike had been another large-scale battle, even more intensive than the one two weeks earlier, with both sides throwing all they could into the encounter, including new weapons. On this occasion, however, the Wing came off second best. No ships were sunk, and two aircrew were killed (F/Sgt. Garton, Sgt. Owens). Four Torbeaus were also severely damaged, two of these crash-landing at North Coates and another at nearby Donna Nook.

Freddie Gardiner and Dick Vimpany were again flying Torbeau 'H' and were one of the aircraft hit by flak, severing an aileron and causing one engine to cut out. They crash-landed at Coltishall, with Vimpany recalling that '*Gardiner did wonderfully well to get us back to England, especially as he was wounded by enemy fire*'. Gardiner did not tell his navigator about the wound until they had landed. The ORB, in its usual matter-of-fact style, referred only to the *slight shrapnel wound in right thigh* incurred by the pilot, although it was serious enough to put Gardiner out of action for nearly a month.

---

2   Nesbit, *The Strike Wings*, p.64.

First use of rockets, on the Strike of 22 June off the Hague; the initial 60lb projectile was difficult to aim and few hits were recorded, as these photographs. (top one taken by Dick Vimpany) demonstrate. (Photos: Crown Copyright/ Vimpany archive & Air Historical Branch)

On 27 July a 254 Squadron Beaufighter achieved the squadron's first 'kill' of an enemy aircraft. Taking off on a dawn reconnaissance mission, S/Ldr. Filson-Young and his navigator P/O Stanley in Beaufighter 'V' were patrolling the Dutch coast at low level when they saw a Dornier 24 search-and-rescue seaplane around 4,000 yards away. Filson-Young closed the range and opened fire at 800 yards, attracting return fire from the Dornier. A second burst from the Beaufighter silenced the enemy's fire, and the Dornier subsequently *'burst into flames and plunged into sea'*. Filson-Young and Stanley then continued their patrol for another 30 minutes before heading back to North Coates.

2 August 1943: Back to winning ways

Wing Strike off Texel

Attacking force		Operating conditions	
Torbeaus:	12 from 254 Sqn	Take-off time:	10:31
Anti-Flak:	14 from 236 Sqn	Flight Duration:	2 hrs 30 mins
	10 from 143 Sqn	Cloud:	Variable
Commanded by:	W/Cdr. Wheeler	Visibility:	8-12 miles
Escort:	51 Spitfires	Wind:	15-25 mph

Several Strikes had been launched during July but had not been successful, the Wing failing to sink any German ships. On 2 August, however, the next big battle took place, with eighty-seven British aircraft engaging nineteen German ships.

The Strike was ordered following a dawn reconnaissance patrol by Gardiner and Vimpany, in Torbeau 'X', who sighted a large convoy near Terschelling. Having taken off at 04.45, they photographed the ships at 06.25, returning rapidly to North Coates at 07.40. The convoy comprised seven merchant ships, all carrying iron ore and flying anti-aircraft balloons, accompanied by four minesweepers, seven flak-ships and a harbour defence vessel. This was a large, well defended group and it responded to Torbeau 'X' with *'uncomfortably close'* flak. Anticipating a Strike later in the day, the convoy alerted the Luftwaffe, which dispatched patrols of four Me109 fighters to provide air cover.

The Wing was in the air at 10:30 and found the convoy an hour later. 236 and 143 Squadrons were armed with 60 lb RP as well as cannon. The attack was mounted from the west, achieving an element of surprise against the ships sailing towards the rear of the convoy. More proficient now with their rockets, the anti-flak force attacked the flak ships of the starboard column, scoring hits on five of these escorts. The Torbeaus of 254 Squadron then made their runs and, although several torpedoes were thought to have grounded on the shallow seabed, two hit the merchant ship *'Fortuna'* of 2,700 tons, which blew up and immediately sank. One of the flak ships also suffered a torpedo hit and sank later, and another was badly damaged.

Pair of Torbeaus on their run, firing cannon, following closely behind another pair which has just passed over the target vessel, off Texel on 2 August 1943. (Photo: Crown Copyright/AIR 28/595)

The patrolling Me109s attacked two of the Torbeaus, a highly courageous action considering the size of the British fighter escort, and the Spitfires claimed to have shot down all four Me109s. Several Beaufighters were hit by flak and two were damaged by the Me109s before the Spitfires could intervene, one crash-landing at Coltishall. However, no Beaufighters or Spitfires were lost and there were no aircrew casualties. The remaining ships of the convoy retreated into Den Helder harbour.

This was the first Strike that John Care and his navigator George Cox took part in, flying Torbeau 'R', and Care pasted two short newspaper clippings into his diary, one of which quoted the Spitfire Wing Leader, W/Cdr. 'Laddie' Lucas remarking that *The low-level attack by the Beaufighters was terrific ... it was thrilling to see one vessel blown sky-high.*[3]

Review of the Strike Wing – its future called into question

On 8 August the Air Officer Commanding Coastal Command, Sir John Slessor, who had taken over from Joubert in February 1943, wrote to the Air Ministry stating that in his opinion the anti-shipping operations off the Dutch coast could no longer be justified in light of the results being achieved. He wanted to break up the North Coates Wing and deploy its squadrons into other areas.

While this view would have surprised the front-line personnel at North Coates, it is more understandable from the perspective of a Commander

---

3   Care archive.

seeking to achieve a wide range of objectives with finite resources at his disposal. And after a good start, the success rate of the Strike Wing had undoubtedly slowed.

In the four months since the start of Wing operations in early April, a total of ten Wing Strikes had been launched against German convoys. Five of these had resulted in sinkings of merchant ships, with a total of six merchantmen and five escort vessels sunk, for the loss of only two aircraft. Five Strikes had not been successful, the Wing either being unable to attack, or attacking and failing to score hits, and losing a total of four aircraft. Overall, the sinking of eleven German ships for the loss of six Beaufighters was seen as a good result, especially in light of the loss rates suffered earlier in the war. (These casualty figures exclude the crews lost in the hunt for the *Nurnberg* and losses during solo sorties and non-operational flying.)

The issue that concerned Slessor was that the Wing's success rate had reduced substantially over the summer. In the two months before 13 June, four out of the five Strikes launched had been successful. In the two months since then, only one out of the five Strikes launched had sunk German ships. This was not due to any lack of effort or resolution on the part of the Strike Wing itself, but because the number of available targets was reducing. Coastal Command's plans had assumed a rate of five Strikes per month whereas only half that number were now being launched.

Slessor was also concerned that even following successful strikes, and when no crews were lost, there was substantial damage to aircraft, which made a high proportion of the Wing unserviceable for some days after the operation. This meant that they would not be available to attack a higher priority strategic target, such as a German capital ship breaking out, if the need for this ever arose shortly after a convoy strike.

The North Coates Strike Wing represented a major commitment of resources, at the time consisting of 60 aircraft, around 120 aircrew and over 1,000 other personnel. Slessor had gaps elsewhere that he needed to fill, such as anti-submarine tasks in the Bay of Biscay and covering possible breakouts by big German capital ships. He therefore proposed to break up the Strike Wing and redeploy its units.

A conference was convened at the Air Ministry on 20 August 1943,[4] with all interested parties represented. Two of these expressed strong support for the retention of the Strike Wing. The Ministry of Economic Warfare pointed to the continuing German demand for iron ore in the Ruhr. The RAF's bombing campaign had not succeeded in reducing steel production capacity, so it was vital to keep up the pressure on raw material supply lines, and in particular to continue to reduce the quantity of iron ore delivered into Rotterdam. The MEW presented evidence that over the summer of 1943 these deliveries had been significantly reduced, with North Sea convoys taking significantly longer to reach Rotterdam, and the Germans increasingly using the much less efficient inland canal supply line from its northern ports into the Ruhr. (The canal route from Emden to the Ruhr could only handle

---

4   (TNA) AIR 15/630.

barges up to 1,500 ton, whereas iron ore could be taken up the Rhine from Rotterdam in 4,000 ton barges, and there were no locks.) This was attributed to the increased threat that convoys sailing to Rotterdam now faced, and the reluctance of Swedish ships now to operate into Rotterdam. The MEW wanted this threat level to be maintained.

The second source of support for the Strike Wing came from the Royal Navy Command at Nore, responsible for naval operations in the southern North Sea. In the Navy's view, the Wing's operations were forcing German shipping to move at night, creating opportunities for its motor torpedo boats to attack and sink ships along the Dutch coast under cover of darkness. The Navy said that it could not sustain this successful offensive if it also had to operate during daylight.

It was also clear at the conference that a possible alternative strategy against the German's supply lines, involving precision bombing of German ports by Bomber Command, was not feasible. There were neither the resources available nor the ability to achieve sufficient accuracy to ensure that the target would be put out of action.

The outcome of the conference was a decision to retain the North Coates Strike Wing, with Fighter Command committing to continue to provide escorts unless there was an overriding reason for not doing so, such as a major daylight bombing raid that required all the available fighter resources. Having convened the conference in the belief that the North Coates Wing was *something in the nature of a luxury that we could not then afford*, Slessor was convinced by the data and analysis presented by the MEW in particular. As he reported later *the results achieved by the North Coates Wing were very much greater than they appeared on the surface …. the toll of sunk and damaged enemy ships by no means indicated the full result of their achievements.*[5]

However, Slessor did decide to reduce the size of the Wing temporarily, sending 143 Squadron on detachment to St. Eval in Cornwall, to reinforce the squadrons flying long-range patrols across the Bay of Biscay. 143 Squadron remained on detachment until early 1944, flying 'fighter interceptor', reconnaissance and naval escort patrols.

A new report was introduced, with 16 Group identifying the reasons for aborted strikes. Information presented to the conference indicated that from 18 April 1943 until 2 August the situation had been as follows:

Number of convoy sightings	48
Crews briefed	24
Of these:	
Strikes resulted	10
Aircraft recalled due to weather	4
Aborted due to faulty reconnaissance	5
Cancelled due to lack of fighter cover	2
Convoy ships too small	2

Source: 16 Group Report, 3 August 1943 in (TNA) AIR 15/541

---

5   Slessor Dispatch, (TNA) AIR 15/773.

Half of the 48 convoy sightings did not lead to crews being briefed, due to factors such as the convoy moving out of range, the convoy already having been attacked on the previous day, and likely non-availability of fighter cover.

Strike Wing retained – but fewer targets to strike

Somewhat ironically, the months following the decision to retain the Strike Wing saw only three successful Strikes executed. A total of eight missions at Wing strength and including Torbeaus were launched from North Coates between mid-August and the end of the year, but five of these either failed to find the target convoy or else encountered adverse conditions that meant that no German ships were sunk. The losses and damage that the Germans had sustained over the spring and early summer had made them wary of pushing convoys down to Rotterdam during daylight hours, so the Wing was presented with fewer targets. Sweden was also now very reluctant to expose its ships to the risk of attack by the Strike Wings and after late summer 1943 very few Swedish ships ventured south of Emden. The tide of the battle had turned – and the Strike Wing had become a victim of its own success.

25 September 1943: An exceptionally fierce encounter

Wing Strike off Den Helder

Attacking force		Operating conditions	
Torbeaus:	6 from 254 Sqn	Take-off time:	10:46
Anti-Flak:	9 from 254 Sqn	Flight Duration:	2 hrs 10 mins
	12 from 236 Sqn	Cloud:	Some at 2-3,000 ft
Commanded by:	W/Cdr. Davies	Visibility:	8-12 miles
Escort:	c.30 Spitfires	Wind:	10-15 mph

Two early morning reconnaissance patrols by 236 Squadron had sighted two separate convoys off the Dutch coast, and a Strike was rapidly launched. After searching unsuccessfully for the first convoy, the Wing found the second target, a large convoy of 14-18 vessels, comprising two large and two smaller merchant vessels, well protected by armed trawlers and flak ships.

The Wing comprised six Torbeaus and nine anti-flak Beaufighters of 254 Squadron, along with 236 Squadron in their anti-flak role. Three squadrons of Spitfires from Coltishall provided the fighter cover. (The splitting of 254 Squadron into both torpedo bombing and anti-flak roles was required due to 143 Squadron being detached from North Coates to Cornwall at the time). The 236 Squadron anti-flak Beaufighters were not armed with rockets for this Strike. Before the attack, the Torbeau flown by Cochrane and Hinks returned to base with engine trouble, and one 254 anti-flak Beaufighter also turned back following a seagull strike. This meant that the Wing going into the Strike comprised only five Torbeaus and twenty anti-flak Beaufighters, against at least ten escorts, including a Sperrbrecher. This was therefore definitely not

Beaufighter clearing away after its cannon attack on the minesweeper in the bottom left of the photograph, which is towing three paravanes, on the Strike of 25 September 1943 off Den Helder. (Photo: Crown Copyright/ Air Historical Branch)

a Strike being made with overwhelming force, given the German firepower protecting the convoy.

The five remaining Torbeaus were flown by some of 254 Squadron's best and most experienced crews, including the Squadron Leader, W/Cdr. Cooper and both Flight Commanders, one of whom was Freddie Gardiner, flying with Dick Vimpany in Torbeau 'J'. The least experienced Torbeau crew was that of John Care and George Cox, in Torbeau 'W', flying on their second strike.

The Wing attacked from the West and was met with *considerable heavy and light flak and much tracer*. After the anti-flak Beaufighters had made their diving attack on the escorts, all five Torbeaus launched their torpedoes from heights between 100 and 190 feet, at distances of 1,000-1,200 yards from their targets. The first pair of Torbeaus targeted the second large merchantman but W/Cdr. Cooper's Torbeau was seen to have its port engine on fire as its torpedo was dropped, and the aircraft crashed into the sea, killing the crew instantly.

Torbeaus 'J' and 'W' then attacked the same ship and Dick Vimpany reported seeing two torpedo hits on the large vessel. The fifth Torbeau successfully torpedoed the smaller merchant vessel next in line. A number of the defending armed trawlers and flak ships were hit by other aircraft. The only confirmed sinking was the flak vessel *Neubau* but the ORB records that *photographs show one large and one smaller M/V torpedoed (the latter on fire) three trawlers on fire and Sperrbrecher damaged.* The Strike had therefore succeeded in putting two merchant ships out of action for a considerable time, as well as a number of escort vessels.

The damage to the Beaufighters, however, was significant, the ORB recording that the flak was very accurate. The torpedo attack had been re-briefed when the formation had arrived over the convoy, as the disposition of the escorts had changed since the original briefing. All four surviving Torbeaus has been hit, including 'J' in the starboard fuel tank and 'W' in the starboard wing. In Torbeau 'V' the navigator, F/O Stanley, narrowly escaped death. While photographing the action, flak ripped away his Perspex cupola, destroying the camera he was using and severely wounding him in the face and head.

The Coastal Command Review commented on the attack plan having had to be changed mid-mission but observed that *North Coates has proved that, despite adverse circumstances, a courageous and well pressed home attack will cause immense damage to the enemy.* Although the fierce encounter had been successful, 254 Squadron had lost its CO, W/Cdr. Cooper, along with his navigator, P/O 'Mattie' Kirkup. Cooper had led the squadron successfully over the whole of the intensive spring and summer campaign and had now paid the price. Cooper's replacement, W/Cdr. Darley Miller, arrived the following day, in time to sign the Squadron's September ORB.

Camera of 254 Squadron Navigator F/O Stanley hit by shrapnel during the Strike of 25 September, severely wounding him in the face and head. (Photo: Crown Copyright/Vimpany archive)

October-November 1943: Some further successes, but also losses

Two further Strikes were completed successfully before the end of 1943. The first of these, on 19 October, damaged the *Strasburg*, a 17,000 ton German liner that had been stranded off Ijmuiden since September and was being towed back to port. The attack by 254 and 236 Squadrons was made with cannon and RP only, in the face of an intensive flak barrage from the enemy ships. Numerous hits were observed on the *Strasburg*, its tug and several escorts, but all ships managed to reach port and one Beaufighter from 236 Squadron failed to return (P/O Markel, F/Sgt. Mallinson).

Gardiner and Vimpany had not flown on the attack on the *Strasburg* and nor did they fly on the next strike, on 23 November, this time because they were the crew of the early morning solo reconnaissance sortie that sighted the target. Taking off from North Coates at 06:20, at 07:44 they spotted a convoy north of the island of Ameland, reporting it to be made up of four merchantmen and seven escorts. Visibility was only 1-2 miles and the light poor, unsurprising at eight o'clock in the morning in late November, so Dick Vimpany was unable to get good photographs. They landed back at base at 09:00.

The Wing launched an operation just over an hour later, with five Torbeaus and nineteen anti-flak Beaufighters getting airborne by 10:30 and heading to Coltishall for the rendezvous with their fighter escort. This first mission, however, was aborted due to poor visibility. All aircraft headed back to North Coates except for W/Cdr. Darley Miller who landed at Coltishall, to liaise with the fighter commanders and ensure that everyone was ready if a second Strike could be launched.

Visibility improved during the day and a second Strike was launched early in the afternoon, the same Strike Wing aircraft taking off from North Coates and making a rendezvous with Miller and several Spitfire squadrons over Coltishall. The anti-flak aircraft were armed only with cannon. The convoy turned out to have a significantly larger escort than had been sighted earlier, with a total of twelve escorting ships in all. However, the biggest of the four merchant ships, sailing last in the line, was identified as a large tanker. The Wing Leader decided to concentrate the Torbeau attack on this valuable target, with the anti-flak aircraft concentrating on the escorts on each side of the tanker. As the Wing attacked from the darker, landward side of the convoy the flak was initially light, but rapidly intensified and became increasingly accurate. All five Torbeaus dropped their torpedoes and two hits were seen, which broke the back of the ship, identified later as the tanker *Weissenburg* of around 7,000 tons. Three of the escorts were seen to be badly damaged by cannon fire, two of them being set on fire.

254 Squadron lost three aircraft during the attack, including two of the Torbeaus, and 236 Squadron lost one aircraft. All four crews were killed (F/O Hague, F/O Pavitt, F/O Hattersley, Sgt. Lenton, F/Sgt. O'Connor, F/Sgt. Kirkland, F/Sgt. Potter, Sgt. Williamson). In the melee, a small group of German fighters had appeared, shooting down two of the Beaufighters as they completed their runs, and damaging another before being chased off by the Spitfires. The other two Beaufighters were lost to the accurate flak, and a number of other aircraft were badly damaged, and crews seriously injured.

This was a successful Wing Strike, carried out with skill and determination, with the scale of the losses reflecting the size and importance of the target. During the course of 1943 the RAF had developed an effective anti-shipping capability, but the Germans had responded, and as 1943 drew to a close this was being reflected in the scale and intensity of the battles fought, and in the losses being suffered by both sides. However, the flow of materials into Rotterdam had been very substantially reduced, and the shipping that was still running the gauntlet along the Dutch coast was taking considerably longer to do so, having to move mainly by night and remain under the protection of the anti-aircraft defences at Den Helder and Ijmuiden during the day.

December 1943: Detachment to Predannack

Going after a blockade runner
It was not unusual for some or all of the North Coates Strike Wing squadrons to be deployed 'on detachment' to other stations, in order to carry out special operations. One notable 254 Squadron detachment took place to Predannack in Cornwall in December 1943.

The target was a 'blockade runner', the *Pietro Orseolo* of 6,300 tons, an Italian merchant vessel capable of sailing at 13 knots. Earlier in the year it had brought back to France a vital cargo of 5,000 tons of rubber from ports in Asia occupied by the Japanese and was believed to be preparing for another voyage to the Far East. In late November the *Pietro Orseolo,* now crewed entirely by Germans, was hiding in the waters off the South Brittany coast, having been damaged by an American submarine and a Mosquito of 487 (NZ) Squadron. In mid-December, the ship was found to be anchored off the Ile de Gros and within range of 248 Squadron's Beaufighters based at RAF Predannack on the Lizard Peninsular. However, this squadron was equipped with cannon-only Beaufighters and used primarily for lengthy patrols over the Bay of Biscay, hunting for the Luftwaffe's long-range patrol aircraft.

Coastal Command decided to deploy 254 Squadron's Torbeaus to attack the blockade runner, with 248 Squadron flying in an anti-flak role, although it was neither trained nor equipped for the Strike role. For the 254 Squadron crews this detachment provided an opportunity for a Strike at a time when these were becoming less frequent in the North Sea, although it also meant leaving their happy home base with Christmas approaching!

An initial detachment of four aircraft had gone to Predannack earlier in December and had flown on a sortie, without sighting a worthwhile target. A further detachment of seven Torbeaus arrived in Predannack on 13 December, and over the following week three armed sorties were launched, with the Torbeaus accompanied by the Beaufighters of 248 Squadron. The operations were all led by W/Cdr. Miller of 254 Squadron flying in an anti-flak role, as the CO of 248 Squadron had no Strike Wing experience. The Torbeaus were led by Freddie Gardiner, flying as usual with Dick Vimpany.

The first two sorties were unsuccessful, failing to find the target and on the second occasion turning back after running into fine weather. The Wing had no fighter escort, and so pushing on in those conditions would have exposed the attacking formation to German single-seat fighters operating from bases along the French coast.

Successful Strike

On 18 December, a third sortie was launched, with orders to press on to the target regardless of the weather conditions. The Wing comprised six Torbeaus led by Gardiner and six anti-flak Beaufighters led by Miller in the Wing Leader role. For this sortie, eight Typhoons from 183 Squadron, also based at Predannack, provided fighter support.

Approaching over the Atlantic from the south-west, this time the Wing found the *Pietro Orseolo,* at anchor off Concarneau, escorted by several anti-flak minesweepers. The attack was launched in classic Wing Strike style, with the anti-flak Beaufighters making what was described as *a single ferocious pass* that severely damaged the blockade runner's superstructure. The Torbeaus then dropped their torpedoes from a height of 100-120 feet and scored two hits, possibly three according to Dick Vimpany's logbook, and the vessel was crippled. The Typhoons, apparently disappointed by the non-appearance of German fighters, joined in and strafed the beleaguered ship.

Fuzzy photograph of the Pietro Orseolo, which has just been hit by a torpedo dropped by a 254 Squadron Torbeau, off Concarneau on 18 December 1943. (Photo: Crown Copyright/AIR 15/471)

Two Beaufighters suffered some flak damage, including from shore batteries, but all aircraft landed safely, three hours and ten minutes after taking off. There were no casualties. The *Pietro Orseolo* was towed to a sandbank where she exploded and sank several days later. John Care flew in Torbeau 'Y' and in his diary described this mission as '*the finest job that 254 Squadron has ever performed*'.

Christmas ruined – the CO complains

The Predannack detachment concluded somewhat strangely – on 24 December the remainder of 254 Squadron's Torbeaus were also sent to Cornwall!

On Christmas Day 1943 the Squadron was dispatched on a *Strike against 2 M/V and 8 Narvik class destroyers in the bay*. One of the merchant ships was believed to be another blockade runner, the 7,000 ton *Orsono*, being escorted towards port with another valuable cargo of rubber. The attacking force was made up of fifteen aircraft from 254 Squadron, including Torbeaus, and more than 20 other Beaufighter and Mosquito aircraft, from 248 and 157 Squadrons, as well as Beaufighters from 143 Squadron that was on detachment at Portreath in Cornwall. This was a large force, comprising more than 50 aircraft, and all the squadrons flew into Predennack for the joint briefing.

The strike force took off, formed up and then ranged far out into the Bay of Biscay. However, the only sightings were of a couple of fishing boats, and the formation headed back to Predannack. Dick Vimpany and some other 254 Squadron navigators believed that the Wing had been turned back too early, before they reached the target area, but they had to maintain radio silence. The 143 Squadron ORB explains the early return as being due to *bad weather conditions expected at base on return.*

The Torbeaus landed at 17:15 in near darkness, four hours after setting out. It was a dreary end to their Christmas Day. Not only had the crews missed out on their Christmas dinner back home at North Coates, but they were also unimpressed at what was left of dinner at Predannack. Ironically the *Orsono* was sighted several days later beached on the French coast, apparently having struck a wreck. 254 Squadron returned to North Coates on New Year's Eve 1943.

It seems that Coastal Command's 19 Group, responsible for the western end of the Channel and the Bay of Biscay, had wanted to take full advantage of the squadron of Torbeaus temporarily at their disposal, but not always in ways that met with the approval of the Squadron's CO. At the end of the month W/Cdr. Miller expressed his frustration about this detachment when signing off the Squadron's monthly ORB Summary.

GENERAL REMARKS BY COMMANDING OFFICER
The month was a difficult one for the squadron, since the Maintenance Plan does not lend itself readily to detachments. The Predannack detachment seriously interfered with squadron training and other operations and was remarkable also for the lack of knowledge on the part of No.19 Group, in the procedure and work involved in briefing a large anti-shipping strike. As a result, the operations from Predannack were considerably handicapped, and matters were not improved by the squadron being ordered out to attempt to locate and destroy a solitary destroyer, reported 300 nautical miles from base:- NOT a torpedo target. Only the intervention of bad weather prevented this quite useless strike leaving the ground.

Someone further up the chain of command was clearly not impressed by Miller's comments and he left 254 Squadron shortly afterwards. He was succeeded as CO by W/Cdr. R.E. 'Paddy' Burns DFC in early January.

'Armed Recces' in early 1944

The success of the Wing during 1943 had reduced the number of targets available for planned Strikes, with convoys sheltering in the heavily defended ports during the day and sailing between these at night. This shortage of Strike opportunities was exacerbated by the onset of winter, with fewer hours of daylight and weather conditions frequently unfavourable. Reconnaissance patrols were flown daily from North Coates when the weather permitted, roaming far along the North Sea coast of Holland and Germany, but convoy sightings that enabled a Wing Strike to be organised became much less frequent.

To maintain the offensive pressure therefore, the Wing began to conduct more armed 'Recces' or 'Recces-in-force'. These involved the Wing going out fully armed in search of targets of opportunity, operating in strength and usually with a fighter escort. While these speculative missions often failed to find a target that could be attacked, several did lead to Strikes on German shipping during the early months of 1944.

One opportunity occurred on 28 January, when ten Torbeaus, six anti-flak Beaufighters and twenty-six Typhoons found and attacked three small vessels nearing Borkum. The attack was not successful, with none of the ships sunk and one Torbeau and one anti-flak Beaufighter lost. One of these aircraft was seen by another crew as being *blown over on side as though by explosion* and crashing, while the second was observed crashing into the sea *without tail unit and chunk out of wing*. (Aircrew fatalities were Flight Sergeants Yates, Tugwell, Lynch and Jukes.)

A mission early in the morning of 21 February achieved better results, with the Wing catching a convoy of 12–14 ships turning into Den Helder at the end of their overnight run. The Wing was back at full strength, 143 Squadron having returned from its long detachment in Cornwall. The force comprised twelve Torbeaus of 254 Squadron and 28 anti-flak Beaufighters from 236 and 143 Squadrons, all escorted by two Squadrons of long-range Spitfires. The sky was swarming with aircraft but although several Torbeaus were 'crowded out', most of them managed to get a clear run in and drop their torpedoes. Gardiner and Vimpany were flying in Beaufighter 'J' and attacked the largest merchant ship, but Vimpany reported seeing their torpedo jump out of the water and dive back in again, missing the target. One torpedo hit was seen on another ship, and it was later confirmed that one of the escorts had been sunk and a number of the other ships in the convoy damaged by cannon fire. One aircraft from 143 Squadron was hit by flak and reported by a 254 Squadron crew as making a *good ditching*, with one of the downed airmen seen in the dinghy. However, both crew members, who were on attachment from 618 Free French Squadron, were later confirmed as killed (Sergeant Pilot Caron and F/Sgt. Pollard).

Another successful sinking was achieved just over a week later, on 1 March. A Recce-in-force in the morning, led by W/Cdr. Burns and comprising nine Torbeaus and fifteen anti-flak Beaufighters, sighted a merchant ship being towed towards Den Helder by two tugs, surrounded by five or six escorts. An attack was made using cannon only and much damage was inflicted on the merchantman, identified as the *Maasburg*, a Dutch ship of 6,000 tons, as well as to several of the escorts. The convoy seems to have been taken by surprise and flak was initially light, developing in intensity only as the attack was already under way, and no aircraft were lost.

It was decided to attack again late in the afternoon and after the aircraft had been refuelled and re-armed a second set of crews set out, consisting of five Torbeaus led by Freddie Gardiner and twelve anti-flak Beaufighters from 236 and 143 Squadrons. The *Maasburg* was sighted just after 17:30, abandoned by its tugs and escorts and lying low in the water. Flak was

Looking back at the torpedo hit on the *Maasburg*, off Den Helder on 1 March 1944. (Photo: Crown Copyright/AIR 15/472)

negligible and the Torbeaus dropped three torpedoes, scoring one hit, the others being reported as near misses. The ship also suffered substantial damage from cannon attacks and was left still just afloat, but clearly in imminent danger of sinking. It was finally sent to the bottom a little later by a Wellington bomber.

Another large armed Recce was flown on 7 March and found and attacked a convoy of eight small ships off the island of Norderney, one of the most easterly of the string of islands patrolled by the North Coates Wing. The attacking force consisted of twenty-four Beaufighters armed only with cannon, drawn from all three of the Wing's squadrons and led by Paddy Burns, and six Torbeaus led by Freddie Gardiner. Five torpedoes were launched but no hits were scored, although all the ships were damaged by cannon fire, with Dick Vimpany recording in his logbook *nine ships, all pranged*. One Torbeau and one anti-flak aircraft failed to return from this four-hour long mission (F/O Walker, F/Sgts. Helps, Smith and McPherson).

Some insight into the importance of tactical discipline was provided by the CO of 143 Squadron, Sam McHardy, who in the ORB observed, *F/Sgt. Newport on his first strike turned back and attacked again and was badly hit in engine and fuselage but returned safely having learnt a good lesson.* Newport had shot down a Ju88 in December and shared with his CO in the destruction of another, and his over-enthusiasm on this Strike did not prevent him being commissioned shortly afterwards. However, he and his navigator, F/Sgt. Slater, were killed in May when their aircraft crashed during a night bombing training exercise.

The run in – armed escort trawler being hit by cannon fire from Gardiner and Vimpany's Torbeau, on the Armed Recce of 7 March 1944 off Borkum. (Photo: Crown Copyright/Vimpany archive)

Looking back – no torpedo hit, but target left damaged by cannon on Armed Recce of 7 March 1944; Vimpany noted later on the print *Strike off Borkum. Own picture after our attack*. (Photo: Crown Copyright/Vimpany archive)

Freddie Gardiner was awarded the DFC on 10 March 1944 and completed his tour of duty with 254 Squadron at the end of that month, but not before leading six Torbeaus on one last mission that resulted in a successful Strike, on 29 March. Accompanied by 22 anti-flak Beaufighters, the Torbeaus attacked a convoy of sixteen small merchant vessels sailing in two columns, accompanied by four escorts, including a Sperrbrecher.

Torpedo hits were reported on two of the merchantmen, the *Hermann Schulte* of 1,305 tons and the *Christel Vinnen* of 1,894 tons, both of which were later confirmed to have been sunk. A number of other ships were damaged, Dick Vimpany observing *at least four ships smoking* and the 143 Squadron ORB reporting a large explosion and *water and smoke rising to 200 ft*. However, one Beaufighter of 236 Squadron crashed into the sea, and the crew were killed (P/O Platten, F/O Johnson).

Gardiner and Vimpany flew together for the last time on the following afternoon, 30 March, when they were part of a full-strength Wing with fighter escort on a Recce-in-force to Den Helder. On this occasion the merchantmen they were seeking had not yet left the harbour, and so were beyond the reach of the Wing, which had to return to base.

Three other attacks during Recce-in-force missions were mounted in April, but no merchant ships were confirmed as sunk. May and early June saw few large-scale engagements against merchant convoys. In the weeks before and after D-Day, on 6 June 1944, the Wing's primary task was switched to

A trio of anti-flak Beaufighters pound an enemy ship with rockets and cannon on the Strike of 29 March 1944. (Photo: Crown Copyright/Air Historical Branch)

that of hunting for E-boats along the Dutch coast at night, to minimise the risk of these fast craft launching attacks on the flank of the invasion fleet. 236 Squadron was detached to Manston in Kent and succeeded in sinking several E-boats and small minesweepers during this period, using cannon and rocket projectiles. On 12 June 236 Squadron enjoyed some target practice when its Beaufighters sank a British tank landing craft, left damaged and abandoned after D-Day but still afloat and judged to be a hazard to shipping.

15 June 1944: The biggest show so far

Wing Strike off Borkum

Attacking force		Operating conditions	
Torbeaus:	10 from 254 Sqn	Take-off time:	04:10
Anti-Flak::	4 from 254 Sqn	Flight Duration:	3 hr 55 mins
	5 from 236 Sqn (RP)	Cloud:	7-9/10,000 feet
	12 from 455 Sqn	Visibility:	5-10 miles
	11 from 489 Sqn	Wind:	15 mph
Commanded by:	W/Cdr. Gadd		
Escort:	10 Mustangs		

On 15 June 1944 an opportunity arose for the North Coates Wing to join forces with the Langham Wing to mount the biggest 16 Group Wing Strike of the war. On the previous day, precise intelligence had been received from the Dutch Resistance that two important vessels had left Rotterdam. These were the *Coburg*, a 7,900 ton experimental ship previously known as the *Amerskerk*, and the *Nachtigalle,* a heavily-armed 3,500 ton E-Boat Depot Ship. The *Coburg* had been the target of the very first Wing Strike, in November 1942, in which three Beaufighters and their crews had been lost without inflicting any significant damage on the ship.

Both enemy vessels had undergone a re-fit at Rotterdam and were making a dash up the Dutch coast, on their way to a deployment in the Baltic. Their escort consisted of a seven large and ten small minesweepers, most flying balloons. Reconnaissance flights confirmed the intelligence, and the decision was made to launch a Strike against this target very early the following morning.

This Strike was carried out by a total of 42 Beaufighters, drawn from both the North Coates and Langham Wings. RAF Langham was on the north coast of Norfolk and the Wing there comprised two Beaufighter squadrons, 455 (Australia) and 489 (New Zealand).

The North Coates Wing took off at 04:10, to rendezvous with the Langham aircraft 20 minutes later, the combined force then picking up their escort of ten Mustangs over Coltishall. These aircraft were from 316 Squadron, the pilots all Polish.

The Strike was led by W/Cdr. Tony Gadd, the highly experienced Wing Commander/Flying at North Coates, who was allocated one of 254's Beaufighters for the mission. W/Cdr. Paddy Burns led the ten Torbeaus. Dick

Vimpany was flying on this Strike with F/Lt. Don Ford DFC in one of the 254 aircraft armed only with cannon. John Care and George Cox were flying in Beaufighter 'V', also with cannon only.

After leaving the coast, Gadd led the force down to sea level, to stay below German radar, and maintained radio silence. The anti-flak aircraft were leading, echeloned out on either side of Gadd's section, with the Torbeaus tucked in behind. However, the formation soon encountered some heavy cloud and fog, and Gadd led his Beaufighters higher and put more space between them, preferring to risk alerting the enemy, rather than letting the formation break up and possibly have to abandon the Strike. Burns kept his Torbeaus low, not wanting to risk getting mixed up with the anti-flak aircraft with visibility so low.

When the fog and cloud cleared, near the Dutch coast, Burns' Torbeaus were all still with him, but he had lost all contact with Gadd's formation and by ill luck his radio had malfunctioned. Just as he spotted the convoy and decided to press on with the attack in spite of the lack of anti-flak support or covering fighters, Gadd's Beaufighters appeared – and Burns' radio came back to life.

By a combination of brilliant navigation and airmanship, and accurate intelligence and plotting of the location of the convoy, despite not being in contact the two sections of the Wings had arrived almost simultaneously at the point from which the attack was to be launched.

Being able to hear Gadd's order to attack, and to communicate with his own force, Burns could hold the Torbeaus back, as the other thirty-two

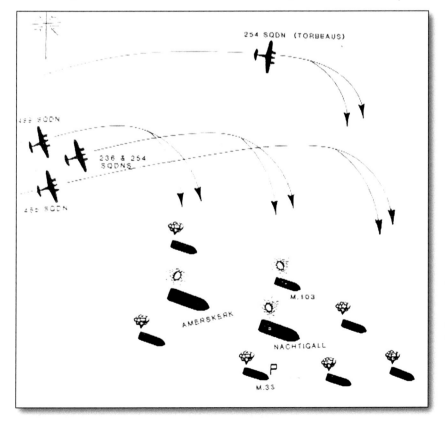

The biggest 16 Group show of the war: diagram illustrating the early morning attack on the *Coburg* and *Nachtigall* and their escorts by the combined North Coates and Langham Wings off Borkum on 15 June 1944. (Based on diagram in Nesbit, *The Strike Wings*)

Beaufighters dived out of clouds to pound the ships with rockets and cannon shells. 455 Squadron attacked the escorts leading the convoy, while Gadd, leading the 236 and 254 Squadron anti-flak aircraft, attacked the minesweeper closest to the *Nachtigalle*, in the centre of the convoy. 455 attacked the escorts and the *Coburg*, sailing at the rear.

The scale and aggression of the flak suppression attack gave the Torbeaus a clear run in, with 236 Squadron's rockets causing the minesweeper protecting the *Nachtigalle* to explode and start to sink just as the Torbeaus were levelling off to launch their torpedoes. All of the other six M-class minesweepers were damaged in the initial attack.

Attacking in their usual 'fluid pairs', six Torbeaus targeted the *Coburg*, which was hit twice. It had already been holed below the waterline by rockets, and it quickly sank. The remaining Torbeaus attacked the *Nachtigall,* which was hit by at least one torpedo. Its stern broke away and it sank later that day, in spite of efforts to tow it into shore. Another torpedo hit a minesweeper, which managed to struggle back to port, despite being holed in several places.

The *Nachtigall* damaged initially by cannon fire. (Photo: Crown Copyright/AIR 15/472)

The *Nachtigall* subsequently hit by a torpedo; it sank shortly afterwards. (Photo: Crown Copyright/AIR 15/472)

The Strike was a complete success. Three German ships had been sunk, including the two priority targets, and six others damaged, several seriously. All the aircraft returned, most in time for breakfast. Several Beaufighters were damaged, but there were no crew casualties, although the Germans erroneously claimed to have destroyed ten aircraft. In his diary John Care remarked that he *was particularly pleased with this effort, as the minesweeper which I targeted with cannon blew up and sank immediately.*

At a period when most public recognition was being awarded to the massive raids on Germany by Bomber Command, Coastal Command finally received some publicity on the following evening, when Gadd and his navigator, F/O Marrow, flew down to London to give their account of the Strike in a two-and-a-half-minute interview on the BBC Nine O'clock News. For their gallantry, Gadd was awarded the DFC and Burns a Bar to his DFC. Somewhat later, their navigators, Duncan Marrow and Frank Woolley, were similarly decorated.

8 August 1944: A Strike just for the Press

Wing Strike off Egersund (Norway)

Attacking force		Operating conditions	
Torbeaus:	12 from 254 Sqn	Take-off time:	12:25
Anti-Flak:	3 from 254 Sqn	Flight Duration:	4 hrs 30 mins
	13 from 455 Sqn	Cloud:	Patchy
	15 from 489 Sqn	Visibility:	4-8 miles
Commanded by:	W/Cdr. Burns	Wind:	Light, variable
Escort:	48 Mustangs		

Publicity can have its drawbacks. After the success of the big Strike on 15 June, in which Australians, New Zealanders and Poles had taken part, the Ministry of Information requested that a similar 'multi-national' mission be mounted on 8 August, this time also including the US Air Force, flying the escorting Mustangs. Up to 40 reporters and photographers were assembled at North Coates to observe the briefing and watch the Beaufighters leave, then to await their return and observe the debriefing.

Unfortunately, no enemy ships of any kind could be found off the Dutch coast, so 16 Group decreed that the mission should be an opportunistic Recce-in-force to Stavanger in Norway, where some ships had been sighted that could potentially form a target. The thirty-eight Beaufighters from North Coates and Langham made their rendezvous with the escort of forty-eight long-range US Mustangs, and all set out on the longer than usual flight to the target area.

Surprise was difficult to achieve, due to small German 'sighting' vessels stationed along the route, as well as the failure of the American fighter escort to maintain radio silence, their objective being to lure up Luftwaffe fighters to engage. A convoy was indeed found but it was well located defensively, the five merchant ships grouped together close inshore, their bows pointed seawards to present as small a target as possible and protected by anti-aircraft batteries on land. The escort vessels included a Sperrbrecher and were positioned to seaward, between the attacking aircraft and the merchantmen.

The small target area meant that the Beaufighters could not all attack at the same time, so that the defensive fire would all be concentrated on a small number of aircraft, as each wave made its run. As well as the usual anti-aircraft guns, the German defensive weapons here included mines dangling from parachutes. Only 40 Mustangs remained with the Beaufighters by this time.

The attack was pressed home aggressively, all twelve Torbeaus dropping their torpedoes, but no hits were observed. Five escorts were badly damaged by rockets and cannon fire, and one sank later that day. The merchantmen escaped unscathed. Three Beaufighters were lost to flak, although one pilot survived ditching in the sea and was taken prisoner when he made it ashore. (The North Coates aircrew killed were S/Ldr. James and P/O Reynolds). A number of Mustangs also failed to return, mainly due to mechanical malfunction.

The assembled journalists were on hand to see the attacking force land back at North Coates. A number of aircraft had been badly damaged, and this excited comment, as did the spectacular crash landing of the last aircraft to return, badly damaged. Despite this, the Strike garnered only two pieces in national newspapers, both of just 150 words. There were obviously far more interesting and exciting actions elsewhere to report, and the Strike Wings slipped back into their former state of obscurity. Burns considered this Strike to be the least worthwhile of all those that that he led.

Although no target could be found for the pre-planned Strike on 9 August, just days later, on 13 August, a large-scale Recce-in-force that included aircraft from Langham and a Spitfire escort, sighted a convoy of 15 ships close to the shore near Den Helder, including merchantmen in two columns. Seven of the 254 squadron aircraft were carrying torpedoes and these executed a low-level attack after what the ORB described as *a gentle glide from 3500 ft*. Only one *doubtful* hit was reported, although the cannon attack did much damage. Flak was heavy from both the ships and the islands offshore, and John Care and George Cox in Torbeau 'V' were caught in a crossfire between two escorts when making their torpedo run. Their aircraft was hit in the starboard engine and a fire started in the fuselage between the pilot and navigator. Cox put out the fire and Care nursed the aircraft back to crash land at Donna Nook. This was their last active operation before the end of their tour, and both men were awarded the DFC.

September 1944-March 1945

The Wing has the upper hand
The absence of a suitable target off the Dutch coast for the publicity-inspired Strike on 8 August was indicative of the broader strategic situation in the Hook-to-Elbe sector of the North Sea. The Germans had stopped trying to send large-scale convoys down the Dutch coast into Rotterdam during

A 236 Squadron Beaufighter on patrol. (Photo: Crown Copyright/Vimpany archive)

daylight hours, and Rotterdam was increasingly defunct as a port. The North Coates Wing had succeeded in 'driving the enemy off the sea' and in practice they were now a deterrent, to ensure that the enemy stayed off the sea.

Numerous Recces-in-force were launched along the Dutch coast, including joint operations with the Langham Wing. A number of these resulted in Strikes at Wing strength, sinking and damaging a number of escorts. Many sorties found no enemy ships, or else failed to catch them outside the heavily defended ports which they sailed between at night. One Recce-in-force was going in to attack a '*passenger type vessel*' on 3 September when it was realised that the target was a hospital ship, and the Beaufighters broke away, but not before coming under fire from shore-based anti-aircraft guns.

A new tactic was developed using single aircraft as 'outriders' from the main force, reporting potential targets by radio to the main force, which could then home in on the target. This was an effective way of expanding the area that could be covered on a Recce, and there was now much less risk of the solo outrider aircraft being attacked by German fighters. This tactic could bring the whole Wing into action over a target much more quickly, denying the convoy the opportunity to run for port, and was adopted widely by all the Strike Wings. But the problem remained – there were now far fewer worthwhile targets available to the North Coates Wing.

Staying on the offensive

The lack of available targets and resulting decrease in the number of ships being sunk and damaged by the Wing meant that there was pressure to re-deploy some or all of the Wing's resources to other areas. 16 Group made a strong case for the retention of the Wing to act as a deterrent and prevent the resumption of German shipping along the Dutch coast, but in October 1944 143 Squadron was transferred permanently to Scotland. Pressure from above remained, however, for the Wing to demonstrate more tangible results.

As well as sailing as far as possible by night, one of the responses developed by the German ships was to run for the shelter of the nearest port as soon as they had been seen by British aircraft. Unless they had been spotted by an outrider the Germans realised that there would normally be three to four hours between the departure of the reconnaissance aircraft and the arrival of the Strike Wing, and they would therefore use this time to seek shelter. Den Helder was a favoured anchorage, heavily defended by anti-aircraft guns. Coastal Command had made several requests for it to be bombed, but Bomber Command refused to consider it as a priority target for its heavy bombers.[6]

In spite of the evident dangers, in September 16 Group ordered several attacks to be made into Den Helder itself. The first raid was mounted on 12 September, with an attack against 12–14 ships in the anchorage launched by the combined North Coates and Langham Wings, armed with cannon, RP and torpedoes. It was not successful, exposing the attacking force to

---

6   (TNA) AIR 15/541 16 Group correspondence.

the full force of the shore-based anti-aircraft defences. No torpedo hits were observed and no ships sunk, although several were damaged. Two North Coates Beaufighters were lost, including the 236 Squadron CO, New Zealander W/Cdr. Tacon, who had been leading the Wing. His navigator, F/O Wardle, was killed by the flak but Tacon managed to bail out, badly burned, and landed on Texel where he was taken prisoner. The other crew lost were F/O Dowding and F/O Hemy of 254 Squadron.

Another attack into Den Helder was carried out on 23 September, with 254 Squadron teaming up with the two Langham squadrons again. The Beaufighters were accompanied on the mission by a camera unit flying in a Boston bomber. On this occasion the targets were all land-based facilities, not ships. There was also poor coordination between the various attacking groups, including the escorting Mustangs, and the Wing lost formation, with aircraft having to attack individually. F/Lt. Don Ford DFC, with whom Dick Vimpany had flown on several Strikes earlier in the summer, was killed on this operation, along with his navigator F/O Wilcox.

Despite the losses incurred on the first two operations against Den Helder, for little gain, another attack was launched several days later. This attack sank two ships, with torpedo hits being observed on the primary target, but the mission resulted in three aircraft being lost (the North Coates aircrew killed were F/O Shepherd and P/O Knowles) and seventeen others damaged. Due to the high number of aircraft and crews that were being lost or damaged, no further operations of this type were launched during the remainder of 1944. The CO of 16 Group, Air Vice Marshall Hopps, concluded that these were *not the type of operation we can indulge in too often, as almost bound to be a costly affair.*[7]

After October the most frequent ORB report after any Wing operation was '*No shipping seen*'. For the next six months the Wing's operations were to be mainly more of the same, with lots of Recce-in-force and other day and night operations, but none of the major battles against large convoys that had characterised the first fifteen months of the Wing's existence. The Wing had succeeded in its primary objective, denying access to Rotterdam, and forcing the Germans to use less efficient supply routes into the Ruhr. As the Allied armies advanced into mainland Europe, the Germans demolished many of the dock facilities in Rotterdam. The Wing's primary task was complete.

Early in 1945, however, a Strike was launched at Wing strength against shipping sighted in the channel outside the harbour at Den Helder. This mission was to demonstrate again the dangers of operating too close to the enemy's harbour defences. However, once again there was pressure from above to re-deploy the North Coates Wing to Scotland, where the Strike Wing battles along the Norwegian coast were still raging. 16 Group made a strong case for the retention of the Wing, to deter E-boats and midget submarines, but there was still pressure for more offensive action, and so another attack into Den Helder itself was ordered.

---

7   (TNA) AIR 15/541 16 Group correspondence.

The North Coates and Langham Wings about to attack ships inside Den Helder on 25 September 1944; a wall of flak is coming up from the massed ships and from shore batteries. (Photo: Crown Copyright/Air Historical Branch)

The Strike on 17 January was led by W/Cdr. Dave Cartridge, CO of 254 Squadron, and the force comprised 16 aircraft from 254 Squadron armed with cannon only, and 16 aircraft from 236 Squadron armed with cannon and RP. The escort was two squadrons of Spitfires from Coltishall, 602 and 603, all armed with bombs. The target was described in the ORB as a single *large Hansa hull*, protected by three minesweepers and six armed trawlers, as well as the concentrated land-based anti-aircraft defences.

The Spitfires attacked first with their bombs, and the Beaufighters followed them in, firing their rockets and cannon. Hits were seen on the large hull and many of the escorts, with all three minesweepers and three of the trawlers left seriously damaged. The Beaufighters also attacked a flak tower, a bridge, a gun emplacement on the shore, and a radar facility.

However, the Strike Wing paid a high price for inflicting this damage to the ships and shore facilities. Although the squadrons' ORBs reported that the flak defences were initially slow to respond to the attack, there was soon *intense heavy and light flak, very accurate, opened from ships and shore* and six aircraft failed to return, three from each squadron. Many other aircraft suffered damage of varying degrees. Nine aircrew lost their lives, the worst single day of losses for the North Coates Wing (F/Lt. Sutehall, F/Os Holvey, Middlemas, Dugdale, Maton, Warburton and Grey, P/Os Troutman and

The *large Hansa hull* being straddled by rockets on 17 January 1945 in Den Helder; the Wing lost nine aircrew during its attack on this unfinished ship and its escorts. (Photo: Crown Copyright/AIR 15/473)

Evans). Several of the downed aircraft managed to make a crash landing ashore, and three aircrew survived and were taken prisoner.

This was the last time that such an attack was mounted, and indeed was the last time that an operation described as a 'Wing Strike' was launched from North Coates. The Wing did not operate again at full strength until the last week of the war and the 'rampage' over Denmark.

The strategic focus shifts

By the autumn of 1944 the focus of Coastal Command's Strike Wing campaign had moved north, to the shipping lanes off the coast of Norway. Here, the Beaufighters and Mosquitoes of the Banff and Dallachy Wings in 18 Group took up the baton from the Wings on the east coast, fighting some very big and fierce battles against what remained a very active shipping route from Narvik to Germany's Baltic ports.

In October 1944, 143 Squadron began to be equipped with Mosquitoes and was transferred permanently from North Coates to Banff on the north coast of Scotland, to fly under the leadership of the charismatic Max Aitken, commanding the Banff station. The Strike Wing campaign off the Norwegian coast had been transformed by the availability of long-range fighter aircraft to escort the anti-shipping aircraft. The US built Mustang is widely credited with having won the air war over continental Europe from 1943 onwards, having both the range and performance to beat the German fighters over their own territory. This was also the case off the coast of Norway, where the Luftwaffe maintained a strong force of single engine fighters almost until the end of the war. With fighter cover now available, the 18 Group Wings could launch Strikes building on the tactics developed earlier in 16 Group, and in a succession of hard-fought battles they succeeded in sinking a large number of vessels during the last year of the war.

April-May 1945: A Final Flourish

The North Coates Wing saw a flurry of activity during the last two months of the war. This included missions to successfully hunt down and destroy midget submarines along the Dutch coast, attacks on Germany's remaining U-Boats, and two very destructive final sorties down through the Kattegat and the Great Belt in Denmark.

Germany had first deployed midget submarines in early 1944, and these included a two-man variant known as the *Seehund,* and one-man versions known as *Biber* and *Molch.* There had been fears that these could be deployed against the shipping supporting the D-Day landings, and although that did not happen, they were still regarded as a potential threat to British shipping, to be sought out and sunk using cannon and depth charges. The Wing achieved considerable success against these midget submarines, sinking nine during March and April 1945, mostly around the Hook of Holland.

By this time the Wing had started to receive new Mosquito aircraft, some armed with very powerful 6lb cannon, and large formations now generally included a mix of Beaufighters and these Mosquitos. The last Wing Strike of the war that included armed Torbeaus took place on 4 April, when six Torbeaus accompanied by eighteen anti-flak Beaufighters and two Mosquitos were dispatched to attack a convoy of three ships off Borkum. However, the vessels were identified as 'Swedish Relief ships', well lit up, and the attack was called off.

'The Rampage'

The Wing's last two operations took place on 3 and 4 May 1945. Both were launched as a *Search for Enemy Shipping* at Wing strength and their task was to attack any enemy vessels sighted. By mid-April, it was clear that the German war machine was grinding to a halt and that the end of the war in Europe was only days away. The Allies were on the Elbe and the Russians in Berlin. There were almost no German ships of any size in the North Sea and intelligence reports indicated that any remaining German ships were desperately short of fuel.

It might seem strange today that in this situation full-scale attacks continued to be launched against enemy shipping, which would surely all soon be in Allied hands. However, at the start of May reconnaissance indicated a substantial build-up of German shipping in the western Baltic, including U-boats and other naval vessels, all fleeing towards Norway. There was a real fear that these forces could continue to offer resistance from Norway, potentially supported by men and equipment transported in the merchant vessels remaining in the area. The North Coates and Dallachy Strike Wings were deployed to counter this potential threat.

Taking off from North Coates at 14:24 on 3 May, seventeen Beaufighters and two Mosquitoes from 254 Squadron and thirteen Beaufighters from 236 Squadron, armed with rockets as well as cannon and escorted by two squadrons of Mustangs, flew across Denmark, down the Kattegat and through the Great Belt. The 254 Squadron ORB records *Many ships of all descriptions seen and attacked*. The tally of sinkings that day was one U-boat, three merchant ships comprising a total of 8,900 tons, a tanker of 6,400 tons, and a small flak ship. In addition, a large liner, *Der Deutsche* of 11,453 tons and another merchantman were seriously damaged. The Wing landed between 19:15 and 19:40 at Helmond in the Netherlands, which had been set up as a temporary advanced base, designated B-86. The Wing suffered its last loss of the war on this sortie, with Beaufighter 'X' and its crew of Sergeants Scott and Farrington seen to go into the sea on fire, due to the intense flak from the minesweepers defending *Der Deutsche*.

On 4 May the Wing took off from Helmond at 13:48, following their overnight stay there. An outrider aircraft had been sent to reconnoitre the Belt and reported sighting three U-boats and some other vessels at sea, and fifteen ships in Nyborg harbour. The Wing attacked and damaged a number of vessels as the aircraft roamed down the Belt, and then sighted the three U-boats in line astern. These were attacked with cannon and rockets and all three were sunk. All aircraft returned safely to North Coates, the last one landing at 22:31. The operation had lasted nearly eight hours, not only the last but also the longest operation that the Wing had flown during its two-and-a-half year history. There is no mention of the ending of hostilities in the Squadron ORBs. From 5 May onwards, relevant entries are a simple *No operations carried out*. Nevertheless, it was over at last.

5

Operational Life

Although the Wing's primary role was to undertake Strikes against German merchant shipping convoys making their way up and down the Dutch coast, it also carried out a range of other operations. Some of these were necessary in order to bring about successful Wing Strikes against an enemy convoy, whilst others employed different tactics, or aimed at different targets, but all with the overriding aim of winning control over the North Sea and cutting off a key German supply line.

Air Operations

Wing Strikes were not every-day events, their frequency depending on a worthwhile target being identified and weather conditions that allowed flying. In the eighteen months after April 1943, Wing Strikes were launched at the rate of approximately two per month, with around half of these missions resulting in a Strike being made against a convoy. However, few days ever passed without some form of operational flying at North Coates, mainly involving sorties by single aircraft. Dick Vimpany's summary of his operational flying reflected this:

> In all, I flew 45 operational sorties with 254 Squadron, and of these, 11 were successful Wing Strikes on enemy convoys. The remainder of the operations consisted of attempted or abortive Strikes (11) which were unsuccessful for reasons of weather, or poor intelligence, or convoys taking shelter (e.g. in Den Helder). Other operational sorties were flights for single aircraft; these were, for example, reconnaissance flights, anti-E boat patrols, night searches for shipping in conjunction with other aircraft, search and rescue flights for missing aircrews, and anti-U boat searches (for 'Biber' midget submarines).[1]

---

1   Vimpany archive.

He flew on his first Strike on 17 May 1943, and on his eleventh and last Strike on 15 June 1944, just before leaving the Squadron for several months, later returning in a mainly non-flying role.

Aircrews would typically hope to complete a tour of a maximum of 200 flying hours before being rested.[2] As the war progressed and increasing numbers of aircrew were produced by the training establishments, operational tours shortened. Freddie Gardiner's tour with 254 Squadron lasted one year, with Dick Vimpany serving a further three months, having completed a total of 125 hours of operational flying before being rested. He also recorded 347 hours of non-operational flying.

Other routine flying activities included training exercises, often intensive and at night, and air testing of the aircraft's engines, equipment and weapons. There were risks involved even in this non-operational flying, with frequent accidents, often in the vicinity of the North Coates and Donna Nook airfields, and sometimes resulting in crew deaths or serious injuries.

'Rovers' and 'Recces'

The missions known as 'Recces', 'Rovers' or 'Night-rovers' were usually undertaken by single, armed aircraft. If a 'target of opportunity' was found, it could be attacked. However, attacks were rare and the most common ORB entry after a three-hour Rover was *No shipping sighted*. On the other hand, the lone Beaufighter on a Rover could go missing, either falling prey to patrolling enemy fighters, or mechanical failure, or an error of airmanship. For these sorties, the ORB entry simply read *Failed to Return* with a blank space left in the column recording the time of landing.

The objective of the Rover or Recce was to locate and photograph shipping movements, usually close to the Dutch coast, and report these to 16 Group for assessment as potential Wing Strike targets. This reconnaissance information was co-ordinated with intelligence gleaned from messages on German shipping movements intercepted by British Intelligence at Bletchley Park, as well as information received from the Dutch Resistance.

A Strike could be launched rapidly, with the Wing sometimes taking off only an hour after the Recce aircraft had landed at North Coates. This happened on 2 August 1943, when Freddie Gardiner and Dick Vimpany were on a dawn Recce and spotted a convoy near Terschelling, leading to a successful Wing Strike before noon. The same thing occurred on 23 November 1943 when Gardiner and Vimpany, again on a dawn Recce, sighted a convoy of four merchant ships and escorts off the island of Ameland. On that occasion the first wave of the Wing was in the air just an hour and a half after the Recce aircraft had landed.

The hazards for the lone aircraft flying on a Recce or Rover had come home forcefully to Dick Vimpany on 10 June 1943, just a month after he had flown on his first successful Strike. He and Freddie Gardiner were on a Recce in the early afternoon and sighted a large convoy off Borkum, just north of the German port of Emden. They flew up and down the convoy for

---

2   Goulter, *A Forgotten Offensive*, p.154.

several minutes, counting approximately twenty ships in total. However, they then sighted four German Me109 fighters, just five miles away and coming straight at them. The ORB entry about the encounter is a laconic *these were lost sight of after 3 mins.* Dick Vimpany adds more detail: *after we had taken photographs we cleared away to the north, with the German aircraft closing in on us. Fred flew north so as to draw the 109's away from their bases, out to sea, to expend their fuel, which was always limited. The enemy aircraft gave up the chase and we then headed west for England.*[3] Gardiner was a former fighter pilot and his quick thinking got them out of a tight corner.

'Armed Sweeps', 'Conebos' and 'Gilbeys'

As the Strike Wings began to gain the upper hand against the German convoys, these were now forced to sail mostly at night and shelter in defended harbours along the Dutch Coast during daylight. With the opportunities for daytime Strikes in Wing strength significantly reduced, the North Coates Wing was increasingly trained and deployed for a number of other specialist attack roles.

Armed Sweeps were patrols of several armed aircraft, a mix of anti-flak Beaufighters and Torbeaus, usually not accompanied by fighters. (As the Allies achieved a degree of air superiority, the Luftwaffe presented less of a threat to the Beaufighters.) These Sweeps were in effect bigger versions of the Rover, entailing the search of a designated area and destruction of any significant enemy shipping found there. The missions were opportunistic, in contrast to the carefully planned Strike on a previously identified convoy.

At various times, the North Coates Wing was tasked to seek and destroy E-Boats. These were small, very fast, heavily armed German naval craft, deployed all along the coast of occupied Europe and seen as a potential threat to the Allied landing force. These operations were rather unimaginatively termed 'Conebos' and usually carried out by Beaufighters operating in pairs. On an early Conebo operation in November 1943 John Care was flying one of four Beaufighters that sighted and attacked four E-Boats. The aircraft closed to 150 yards and set one E-boat on fire and damaged all of the others. Care commented in his logbook that it was *a day to remember – particularly pleased with my accuracy* but *We lost Bunny Palmer.*[4] F/O Palmer and his navigator F/O Smallwood in Beaufighter 'F' had attacked immediately the E-Boats were sighted, before the other aircraft were in position to make their runs. Although the flak from the E-Boats was described in the ORB as '*intense but not very accurate*', their aircraft was hit and crashed into the sea, killing the crew.

Conebo sorties intensified in 1944 as D-Day approached. Flying with W/Cdr. Paddy Burns around this time, Dick Vimpany records in his logbook that they searched for E-Boats to attack although they found *everything but*, as the E-Boats stayed away from the invasion fleet.

In response to the reduced number of German ships sailing during daylight, a further specialist mission was introduced, code-named '*Gilbey*'. This was a night operation that combined the bombing capability of a Wellington or Avenger aircraft with the torpedo capability of a Torbeau.

---

3   Vimpany archive.
4   Care archive.

Using its radar, the Wellington would search for German shipping along the Dutch coast, often guided by intelligence reports about enemy sailings. If a target was located, the Wellington would call in the patrolling Torbeaus and all the aircraft would launch a combined attack, illuminating the target with a large number of flares and then dropping both bombs and torpedoes. When the tactic was first proposed, the Air Officer Commanding Coastal Command, Sir John Slessor, referred to it a *wild-cat scheme* and asked why the Wellington could not be more usefully employed![5]

The technique was difficult to execute, but achieved some success, making night sailing more hazardous and thereby putting further pressure on Germany's already stretched shipping resources. Freddie Gardiner and Dick Vimpany flew a Gilbey mission on 11 February 1944, but without success. John Care also flew on several unsuccessful Gilbeys in February, including one operation when the Wellington was shot down by an enemy night fighter.

Search-and-Rescue

The response to an aircraft going missing would often be a search and rescue mission by other aircraft from the Wing. Many aircrews were lost as a result of battle-damaged or malfunctioning aircraft ditching in the North Sea. Even following a good ditching and escape from injury there would be only a minute, probably less, to deploy and climb into a dinghy and get clear of the sinking fuselage. The crew would then hope that a friendly search aircraft would spot and report the position and initiate a rescue by an air-sea rescue launch, based at Grimsby, or by some other craft nearby.

Air Sea Rescue was a Coastal Command responsibility and by the end of 1943 it was operating 175 rescue craft, including 114 high speed launches. During 1943 a total of 1,600 airmen were rescued from the seas around Britain.[6]

Dick Vimpany summed up his experiences and his feelings about the various forms of operational flying that he experienced with the North Coates Wing:

> *Although one Strike was very much like another, in that they consisted of a very busy preparation period, an extremely concentrated time of the attack, and then the return flight watching for enemy fighters, the more worrying operations to me were the lone flights in daylight of about three hours and often close to enemy bases. Although losses of aircraft were high on Wing Strikes, especially in 1943 and 1944, many aircraft were missing on these long reconnaissance and search flights by day and night.*[7]

Detachments

Although very much at home at their Lincolnshire base, the North Coates Strike Wing squadrons were often called upon to operate from other Coastal

---

5   (TNA) AIR 15/541 correspondence.
6   Coastal Command Review, December 1943.
7   Vimpany archive.

High Speed Launches. (HSL) based at Grimsby docks and directed from RAF North Coates sped across the North Sea to retrieve survivors from ditched aircraft; the circling aircraft here is waiting until the launch has the downed airmen safely on board. (Photo: Crown Copyright/AIR 15/472)

Command stations in other Group sectors and some of 254 Squadron's crews jokingly referred to themselves as the '254th Light Foot'. An early detachment, of the entire Wing, was to the north of Scotland at the start of May 1943, to participate in the fruitless and costly hunt for the cruiser *Nurnberg*.

Another detachment was that of 143 Squadron to Cornwall, with eleven Beaufighter crews initially spending much of August 1943 flying from St Eval, seeking U-Boats in the Bay of Biscay. This was followed by the whole of 143 Squadron being detached to Portreath in Cornwall for nearly five months, flying long fighter interceptor, reconnaissance, and naval escort patrols, singly and in groups. The squadron did not return to North Coates until early 1944.

Most of these patrols over the Bay of Biscay were without incident, but on two occasions 143 Squadron's Beaufighters engaged in aerial battles with the Luftwaffe. On 12 December six Beaufighters were 'jumped' by five Ju88's, who shot down two of the Beaufighters, killing the crews (F/Lt. Tucker, F/O Scott, F/O Bentley, Sgt. Phillips). In the ensuing dogfight, however, three enemy aircraft were shot down, with no further losses incurred by 143 Squadron. W/Cdr. McHardy, the Squadron CO, and Sgt. Newport claimed one 'kill' each, and they shared the third. On the second occasion, on Christmas Eve, six Beaufighters attacked two He177 long-range bombers and shot one down, for no loss.

The 143 Squadron ORB for December provides some insight into the operational problems caused by detachments. The shortage of ground staff and facilities made it very difficult to maintain aircraft serviceability, and this was only made possible by the *hard work of the ground crew, who are working under adverse conditions, including poor accommodation.* The posting in of two additional fitters was welcomed to help alleviate the maintenance problems, and the efforts of 19 Group to obtain more men and material for the squadron on detachment were recognised.

A successful, if unpopular, detachment was 254 Squadron's participation in the operation against the blockade runner *Pietro Orseolo* around Christmas 1943, described earlier. This mission was launched from Predannack in Cornwall, the Beaufighters flying there from North Coates. Travelling light and at short notice, key ground crew hitched rides in the Beaufighters while fittters, armourers and others were transported by aircraft with their equipment shortly afterwards, not knowing how many days or weeks they would be away from North Coates.

RAF Manston was another forward base for detachments, from where the Wing could cover the English Channel, and 236 Squadron moved there three days before D-Day, in case its Beaufighters were needed to support the invasion. Manston was much closer to North Coates and a detachment there was less of a logistical challenge than a move either to Cornwall or to the north of Scotland.

The North Coates Wing's final detachment was its brief deployment to Helmond airfield in Holland, designated as 'Landing Ground B86', just as the Germans were on the brink of defeat. This was the base from which the Wing launched its last Strikes of the war, against German vessels in the Kattegat on 3 May and 4 May 1945, when it sank four U-boats and four merchantmen.

The Wing returned to North Coates on 4 May, after its brief detachment to continental Europe and last operational mission of the war. Dick Vimpany, however, enjoyed his own personal detachment on 5 May, when he flew to Luneberg to recover some RAF prisoners of war, the day after the formal surrender of the German forces to Field Marshall Montgomery on Luneberg Heath.

Preparing for a Strike;
armourers at North Coates
arm a 254 Squadron Torbeau.
(Photo: Crown Copyright/
Vimpany archive)

Ground Operations

From late 1942 onwards, RAF North Coates, together with its satellite station at RAF Donna Nook, was home to up to 1,500 personnel, mostly in uniform. Of these, around 120 were aircrew attached to the three Strike Wing squadrons, of whom roughly half were commissioned and half non-commissioned. In addition, there were over 1,300 ground personnel, of whom approximately 70 were commissioned officers. Every airman attacking a German convoy was therefore being supported by around ten people on the ground.

The ground crews comprised fitters, armourers, mechanics, electricians, and various other specialists. There was always a good relationship on the Wing between ground crew and air crew, the latter knowing and respecting that they were absolutely dependant on the skill and dedication of the men on the ground to keep their Beaufighters armed and in the air day after day.

Other trades represented among the personnel based at North Coates included cooks and mess staff (officers' 'batmen', some of whom were women), drivers (many of them young women too, serving in the WAAF), clerks and office staff, medics (most bases had their own much used 'sick quarters'), fire personnel and others.

A substantial headquarters organisation was required to keep three squadrons of Beaufighters operational. The HQ officers included the Station Commander, Adjutant, Catering Officer, Engineer Officer, Navigation Officer, Medical Officer, Motor Transport Officer, Accounts Officer, Flying Control Officer, Chief WAAF Officer, Intelligence Officer, Torpedo Officer, and about twenty others, all needed to keep the 120 or so aircrew flying.

RAF North Coates HQ Staff, 30 December 1943. The Station CO, Gp/Capt. Giles Gilson, is seated centre; Flt Lt. George Fern DFM, the Station Navigation Officer. (who had dropped the Tricolour on Paris in June 1942) is seated on the ground, second from right. (Photo: Crown Copyright/Vimpany archive)

254 Squadron, late 1943, comprising aircrew and administration personnel; the CO, W/Cdr. Darley Miller, is seated in the centre with dog; F/O John Care is first left on the back row; F/Sgt. Dick Vimpany is fifth from right on the back row; F/Sgt. Freddy Hinks is sixth from right in the middle row; F/O Arnold Kelshall is seated third from right and F/O George Cox seated fourth from right. Seven of the aircrew in the photograph had been killed by the end of the war. (Photo: Crown Copyright/Vimpany archive)

The North Coates community

With its community of up to 1,500 people, the North Coates base functioned almost as a small town. As well as the good relationships between the air and ground crews, there was also an informality between commissioned and other ranks. In the air, the pilot and his navigator formed a close partnership, their ranks irrelevant. The same was also true to an extent on the ground, where the quality of the work and the commitment were more important than the rank of the man doing it.

At any one time there were about the same number of non-commissioned aircrew (Sergeants and Flight Sergeants) as there were commissioned officers. Many NCO aircrew were commissioned before the end of their first tour was completed (including Dick Vimpany and Freddy Hinks). Men like these were the backbone of the wartime RAF, with many who first flew in combat as 20-year old Sergeants ending their war service several years later commanding flights and squadrons.

Another reason for the lack of formality between ranks prevailing at North Coates was almost certainly the presence of so many aircrews from the Empire and Dominions, which were less class-bound societies and where social attitudes were less instinctively deferential. The 254 Squadron Aircrew Nominal Roll for late October 1943 shows that at least eleven pilots or navigators were from Canada, New Zealand, Australia, Rhodesia, and the USA. At other times there were French, Dutch and Belgian crews flying with the Wing, and one pilot from Trinidad, F/O Arnold Kelshall. The Wing's first leader, W/Cdr. Neil Wheeler, was South African.

All three services had entered the war with a structure based largely on social class and the divisions prevailing in society at the time. The pre-war RAF had attracted many adventurous ex-public schoolboys and university men, eager to be pilots, and at the start of the war there was a disproportionate number of officers from this background flying with the RAF's front-line squadrons. There was also still a tendency throughout the military at that time for the British to look down slightly on 'colonials'.

By the end of 1942, however, there was a much wider cross-section of fliers in the RAF, as reflected in the Squadron rolls at North Coates. The need for many more airmen had brought in experienced pilots from overseas and had widened the opportunities for young men in Britain to train as aircrew. Early in the war many former Grammar School boys had joined the Royal Air Force Volunteer Reserve, to await aircrew training. Two examples were 254 Squadron navigators Dick Vimpany and Freddy Hinks, who had left Lawrence Sheriff Grammar School in Rugby aged sixteen to begin engineering apprenticeships. After joining the RAFVR at eighteen, they both found themselves flying in Beaufighters and, quite coincidentally, were both posted as Sergeants to the same squadron at the age of nineteen. Other Coastal Command aircrew had joined before 1939 as apprentices on the ground staff and were later selected to train as pilots, navigators and flight engineers. By 1943 the Strike Wings were representative of a Royal Air Force with a broad societal base, the evolution towards a less hierarchical organisation being hastened by the exigence of war.

6

The Men Who Led

Neil 'Nebby' Wheeler

Beaufighter Pilot, Commanding Officer 236 Squadron, Wing Commander (Flying) North Coates Strike Wing, 1942–43

Later to become one of the RAF's most distinguished senior officers, Neil Wheeler consolidated the tactical 'conditions for success' that transformed the effectiveness of the Strike Wings after 1942, initiating a rigorous operational training programme and leading the North Coates Strike Wing in battle in 1943.

Wheeler, already a proven air leader, was posted to North Coates at short notice to command 236 Squadron, following the death of its previous Commanding Officer on the Wing's first ill-fated Strike in November 1942. He quickly realised that the Wing's crews had the necessary skills and commitment to mount anti-shipping attacks, and that the Beaufighter was the right aircraft, rugged and reliable and with the range, speed and firepower to take on the well-armed German convoys. Success, however, would depend on intensive training and a strict adherence to coherent battle tactics. Wheeler was respected by his crews as hard but fair, and by the spring of 1943, after a rigorous training programme and with morale restored, the North Coates Wing was ready once again to take the offensive.

W/Cdr Neil 'Nebby' Wheeler – a proven leader, who developed the North Coates Strike Wing into a formidable anti-shipping force. (Photo: Crown Copyright)

On 18 April, Wheeler led the Wing to Texel, where it attacked and sank the largest ship in a heavily defended convoy, scoring three torpedo hits and losing no aircraft. The Wing returned to a jubilant welcome from the North Coates ground personnel, and this Strike marked the start of a period of successful Wing Strikes and mounting German losses. By the time Wheeler left the Wing in September 1943, when he was awarded his second DFC, the Strike Wings held the initiative in the North Sea, with German shipping increasingly denied access to Rotterdam.

Neil ('Nebby') Wheeler was born in Pretoria, South Africa in 1917 and completed his school education in England, winning a scholarship to RAF College, Cranwell.

His college reports did not suggest the full potential of his subsequent successful career as an air commander, but when war came he seized the opportunity to fly Spitfire reconnaissance missions, pioneering low-level reconnaissance tactics. He was recognised as an exceptional pilot and leader, and after fifty-six missions was awarded his first DFC.

In his obituary, The Times described Wheeler as *one of the RAF's most distinguished post-war officers*. He held commands in Malaya during the Emergency, commanded strategic bomber squadrons in the 1950s, became assistant commandant of Cranwell, held senior air staff appointments in Europe and was responsible for the procurement of the Tornado. Retiring from the RAF in 1973, he joined Rolls-Royce and remained an influence within military aviation. Importantly, he also retained links with the survivors of the Strike Wings, often presided over the North Coates Wing Reunions, and led the veterans who were present at the dedication of the Strike Wing Memorial at Cleethorpes in 1999.

Air Chief Marshall Sir Neil Wheeler FCB, CBE, DSO, DFC and bar, AFC, FRAeS died in 2009.

R.E 'Paddy' Burns

Torbeau Pilot, Commanding Officer 254 Squadron, January-September, 1944
Paddy Burns, described in his obituary in The Times as *a charming and witty Errol Flynn look-alike*, took command of 254 Squadron in January 1944.

Burns was born in India in 1912, the son of an Indian Army engineer. He came to England to study engineering at Imperial College, London, and after graduating in 1934, joined the RAF. When based in Palestine in 1936, Burns intervened in the ambush of a British army patrol by strafing and bombing its attackers, enabling the patrol to withdraw. Instead of facing a court martial for disobeying the prevailing 'rules of engagement', on the recommendation of the senior army commander he was awarded a DFC, a rare distinction in the inter-war years.

By the spring of 1941 Burns was in charge of the RAF's Torpedo Development Unit at Gosport, set up to improve the effectiveness of the aircraft torpedo, a field of expertise that had been largely ignored since the end of the First World War.

As Commanding Officer of 254 squadron, Burns led many Wing Strikes and armed patrols. His most accomplished feat of airmanship, courage and leadership was regarded to have been the Strike of 15 June 1944. This was the biggest anti-shipping operation of the war until then, when the North Coates and Langham Wings combined to sink both the major target ships, as well as sinking one escort and severely damaging all six others. Burns led the ten Torbeaus on this Strike, and was awarded his second DFC and promoted to Group Captain shortly afterwards.

W/Cdr Richard 'Paddy' Burns, torpedo expert and effective Torbeau strike leader. (Photo: Vimpany Archive)

After the War Burns remained in the RAF, regaining his wartime rank of Group Captain in 1954. As an engineer, he was involved in the co-ordination of nuclear weapons development with the United States, and later served as the commandant of the famed Empire Test Pilot School at Farnborough.

In civilian life he joined the British Aircraft Corporation. He delivered a lecture in 1978 to the Royal Aeronautical Society, explaining in clear terms the development of the torpedo for aerial use and describing from experience how the Strike Wings deployed these in typical anti-shipping operations. He retained links with former members of the Strike Wings throughout his life.

Group Captain R.E. Burns CBE, DFC and Bar died in 2001.

A. 'Tony' Gadd

Beaufighter Pilot, Wing Commander (Flying), North Coates Strike Wing, 1944

Tony Gadd was one of Coastal Command's most experienced and effective Strike Wing leaders. From Cranbrook School he joined the RAF before the War on a short service commission and trained on torpedo bombers at the Gosport Torpedo Development Unit, becoming an instructor and an expert in torpedo tactics. He was reputed to have dropped over 1,000 dummy torpedoes in experimental trials.

In the summer of 1940, he joined 22 Squadron at North Coates as a Flight Commander, flying Beauforts (serving alongside Patrick Gibbs). He survived his tour, despite the heavy losses that 22 Squadron experienced during this period. He was then seconded to the Royal Australian Air Force as an instructor on torpedo-bomber tactics and was credited with the probable sinking of a Japanese submarine. His next posting, in 1943, was to the Beaufighter Officer Training Unit at East Fortune in Scotland, before arriving at North Coates in mid-1944 as Wing Commander (Flying). On 15 June 1944 Gadd led the forty-two Beaufighters of the joint North Coates and Langham Wing Strike in the biggest 16 Group anti-shipping Strike of the war of the war. It proved a complete success, with the two target ships destroyed as well as one of the escorts, with no loss of aircraft, and Gadd was awarded the first of his two DFCs. He was also interviewed on the BBC News that evening, one of the few occasions on which the Strike Wings received any public recognition.

In August 1944, Gadd moved north to command 144 squadron until the end of the war, based first at Banff and then at Dallachy, and here too he often took on the role of Wing Commander (Flying). His operational tours therefore included service in the pre-Strike Wing Beaufort period, in the Pacific theatre, and in Strike Wings in both 16 Group and 18 Group, a unique record.

Tony Gadd remained in the RAF until 1952. In civilian life he had business interests in coin-operated launderettes and property development in Surrey, where he restored oast houses. Genial and debonair, he was a popular attendee at North Coates Strike Wing reunions. One of Tony Gadd's wartime uniforms is on display in the museum maintained by the Flying Club at North Coates airfield.

Wing Commander A. Gadd DFC and Bar died in 1996.

E.H. 'Sam' McHardy

Beaufighter Pilot, Commanding Officer 143 Squadron, 1943–44

Edric 'Sam' McHardy was a New Zealander from a large North Island farming family. In 1938 he joined the RAF on a short service commission and travelled to England for his flying training, which he completed as a pilot graded 'Excellent' shortly after the outbreak of war. He first joined 248 squadron, which became a Coastal Command unit and moved to RAF North Coates in February 1940. McHardy took part in the hazardous anti-shipping operations over the North Sea and later along the Norwegian coast. Flying the Blenheim as a night fighter, he also saw action with 248 Squadron during the Battle of Britain. He was awarded his first DFC and posted to 404 (Canadian) Squadron as a flight commander in July 1941, continuing to fly on operations over Norwegian waters, including an attack on the battleship *Prince Eugen*. After the award of a Bar to his DFC, between July and October 1942 he commanded 404 squadron He was then posted to Ferry Command, which took him to Africa and South America.

Sam McHardy returned to Coastal Command operations in November 1943 as CO of 143 Squadron, which had just been detached from North Coates to Portreath in Cornwall, following the Strike Wing campaign over the North Sea during the spring and summer of 1943. Following this period of intensive and successful action, the squadron's new long-range patrolling and reconnaissance task over the Bay of Biscay, based at the remote and dreary location of Portreath, was beginning to affect morale. McHardy arrived to hear complaints about aging aircraft and insufficient ground crews, but he immediately injected energy and leadership, ensuring that 143 Squadron remained an aggressive and skilled fighting unit. In December 1943 McHardy shot down a Ju88 and claimed a share in a second during an aerial battle over the Bay of Biscay. His 143 Squadron then re-joined the Strike Wing at North Coates in February 1944.

During the week following D-Day in June 1944 McHardy led six successful attacks on enemy shipping. He was awarded the DSO, before taking 143 Squadron north to Scotland in October 1944 to join the Banff Strike Wing and participate in the successful campaign along the Norwegian coast.

Notably, McHardy completed three tours of anti-shipping operations. He was one of the very few men who flew active anti-shipping operations in Coastal Command in the pre-Strike Wing era and then with Strike Wings in both 16 Group and 18 Group. Sam McHardy was a successful and highly respected example of the many exceptional airmen who joined Coastal Command from the Dominions, and who attained key leadership fighting commands. He remained in the RAF after the War, retiring in 1958 when he returned to New Zealand to work in the wool and financial services industries.

Wing Commander E.H. McHardy DSO, DFC and Bar died in Matakana, New Zealand, in 1990.

F.T. 'Freddie' Gardiner

Torbeau Pilot, Commander 'A' Flight, 254 Squadron, 1943-44

Freddie Gardiner learnt to fly as a schoolboy in Northern Ireland, going solo for the first time at a flying club there in April 1935. He was educated at Stowe School in England and in 1936 entered Cambridge University to study engineering. He joined the University Air Squadron and the RAFVR, training on Avro Tutors and Hawker Harts, and as a pilot was known as 'steady Freddie'. He was also a member of the university gliding club and was a winner at the 1939 National Gliding Championships. His early flying experiences included at least two emergency landings when his aircraft developed mechanical problems.

When war broke out, much to Gardiner's annoyance the entire university squadron was called up to do their basic training over again at RAF Cranwell. After graduating, Gardiner completed the conversion course on Hurricane fighters and then Spitfires, joining 610 Squadron on 16 June 1940, first at Gravesend and then at Biggin Hill in Kent, in time for the Battle of Britain. His air combats in July and August were nearly all against Me109s. One day, after an early morning operation, he was asleep in a chair in the mess when Winston Churchill made an unofficial visit to the base, on his way to Chartwell. Gardiner did not wake up, afterwards recalling that *Churchill saw me, but I did not see him*. During the Battle of Britain Gardiner recorded one confirmed kill and one 'probable' and was

Frederick 'Freddie' Gardiner – portrait as a Battle of Britain pilot, painted by Eric Kennington, official war artist. (Crown Copyright, reproduced with permission of the Gardiner/Fleck family)

slightly wounded twice, before being shot down on 25 August by *an aeroplane I never saw*. He bailed out near Dover, suffering burns to his face and hands. On landing in a field in Kent, he was taken to hospital in an ambulance sent from the local coal mine. As his parachute was initially observed not to have opened, he was first reported as killed, and some Battle of Britain records list him as killed-in-action [1]

After leaving hospital he returned to his squadron in October, but by then the Battle of Britain was won and soon he was posted for *two uneventful years* as an instructor at a glider pilot training unit. He did, however, recall an incident involving Air Vice-Marshall Sir Keith Park, who had been Commander-in-Chief of 11 Group during the Battle of Britain. Gardiner took Park up to demonstrate glider flying, and having landed safely, was waiting for the tractor ground tow when the towing

---

1   Vimpany Archive and Gardiner/Fleck family papers.

aircraft landed on top of their glider, narrowly missing the Air Vice Marshall's head (and Gardiner's).

In December 1942 Gardiner converted to the Beaufighter torpedo bomber, at No. 2 Coastal Operational Training Unit at Catfoss, Yorkshire and joined 254 Squadron in April 1943. The previous commander of 'A' Flight had just been killed in action and Gardiner immediately stepped into the role, starting an eventful one-year tour with the North Coates Strike Wing.

At Catfoss he had been 'crewed up' with navigator Dick Vimpany, and they flew on 37 operations together over the following twelve months, including 11 Strikes. Their Torbeau was damaged by flak several times, sometimes seriously, and they crash-landed at RAF Coltishall after the aircraft was hit by flak during the Strike of 22 June 1943. In his own brief account about his war service,[2] Gardiner fails to mention that he also received a shrapnel wound during this Strike. Nor does he mention being awarded the Distinguished Flying Cross in March 1944, for *his fine fighting qualities and unfailing devotion to duty*.[3]

Dick Vimpany recalled Freddie Gardiner as a very cool and canny pilot. On one solo Recce flight they found a convoy and photographed it, but as they cleared away they were spotted by the convoy's four escorting four Me109s. With the German fighters closing on them, Gardiner chose to fly north, drawing them further out to sea and away from their bases, to expend their fuel. After four tense minutes the enemy aircraft gave up the chase and turned for home.

Freddie Gardiner. (left) with Dick Vimpany at the Wing's reunion in October 1988. (Photo: Vimpany archive)

2   Vimpany archive and Gardiner/Fleck family papers.
3   *London Gazette*, 10 March 1944.

In April 1944 Gardiner was posted as Wing Commander (Flying) at a training unit for Torbeaus and other aircraft in Egypt, and at the end of the war was he commanding an anti-submarine squadron in Aden, flying Wellingtons. He described this last posting as a *good way to end six years of war*.

After leaving the RAF in 1946, Gardiner completed his engineering studies and emigrated to Vancouver, Canada, where he established a successful consulting engineering business. He retired at the age of 55 and spent much time sailing and cruising. In the 1970s and 80s he made visits to England to see family and wartime friends, including Dick Vimpany, and they attended several Wing reunions together.

In a letter to his old navigator,[4] well after the war, he mentions that he had come across some RAF statistics recording the *Percentage chance of Survival* for different classifications of aircraft. These indicated that one complete tour in Torpedo Bombers offered a 17.5 percent chance of survival whereas one tour in Catalina flying boats offered 77.5 percent. Gardiner's comment to Vimpany was *The advice of 'your man in front' is to avoid torpedo bombers – next time we should do it Catalinas!*[5]

Wing Commander F. T. Gardiner DFC died in Victoria, British Columbia, Canada in 2003.

---

4   Vimpany archive.
5   In fact, these figures relate to Coastal Command operations in 1940-42, before mobilisation of the Strike Wings, on which casualty rates were lower; the Strike Wing casualty rate was in fact similar to that of Bomber Command.

7

North Coates Camp

North Coates Airfield is on the North Sea coast about seven miles south of Grimsby and Cleethorpes. From today's Flying Club control tower one can look east, over the foreshore and towards the coast of Holland, occupied by the enemy in 1943. Little remains today of the buildings and infrastructure that comprised wartime North Coates, although the footprint of the 1940s layout will feel familiar to anyone who has lived or worked on an RAF camp. In 1943-45 it was a place of intense activity and a home and refuge for up to 1,500 young men and women, mostly in RAF or WAAF uniform.

Before 1939

When the First World War began in 1914, the area that became RAF North Coates comprised the fields of two farms. The bleak and exposed terrain, previously known as North Cotes Fitties (this being the original spelling of the place name, and 'fitties' being local slang for salt-marsh), was leased by the Army to serve as a temporary camp for military training. It also provided a convenient landing ground for the Royal Flying Corps and Royal Naval Air Service machines that patrolled the coast searching for enemy aircraft and Zeppelins. Later it evolved into a fully-fledged air station, with officers accommodated in the farmhouses and the enlisted men under canvas. Towards the end of the war the newly formed RAF assumed control of the temporary station, and in the mid-1920's took a new lease to develop a permanent station as a training base and landing ground for aircraft using the bombing range at nearby Donna Nook.

In the 1930s the nationwide programme to expand and upgrade RAF stations meant that the canvas accommodation was replaced by wooden huts, and these were also used to house other facilities such as the NAAFI and workshops. The new buildings were frugally heated, usually by a single coal-fired stove, and raised above the ground to avoid the damp rising from the earth. They were painted camouflage green.

The timber headquarters building, laid out in an 'H' configuration, contained the station administration offices, war operations room, and photographic section. The timber Control Tower was erected by a local builder, and another building housed a Sick Quarters. Two grass runways were in use, with the original east-west runway gradually extended in the mid-1930s, and a north-south runway added shortly afterwards.

The fabric 'Bessonneau' hangars were replaced by four permanent structures, easily identifiable on an aerial image, aligned parallel to the concrete runway. These were unique to North Coates, not replicated at any other RAF airfield. A further three of the more basic 'Bellman' type hangars were built adjacent to the north-south grass runway, with another Bellman added in 1940. All the hangars were camouflaged, patterned green and brown.

Wartime Expansion, 1939-45

In February 1940, the station was brought under the control of 16 Group Coastal Command and the word 'Fitties' dropped from its title. The first Coastal Command unit to arrive was 248 Squadron, equipped with Blenheims, which heralded the start of two years of difficult and costly anti-shipping operations mounted over the North Sea from North Coates. It was at this time that RAF North Coates, now an active front-line base, adopted the motto 'Guide to Attack', a phrase that resonates well with its role both during and after the war.

Aerial view of North Coates airfield, looking inland, taken in 1942 before completion of the concrete east-west runway; the broader north-south grass runway, which could accommodate several aircraft taking off together, extends between the camp and the shoreline. (Photo: Crown Copyright, Vimpany archive)

In 1943 a concrete runway was constructed, extending 1,420 yards west-to-east towards the shoreline, at right-angles to the established 1,460 yards long north-south grass runway. Hard aircraft parking stands were gradually added, as were dumps for bombs, torpedoes and rocket projectiles.

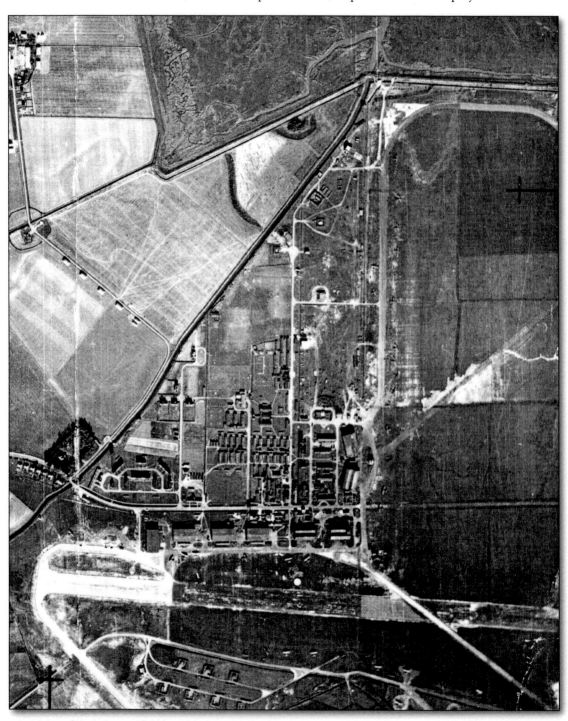

Aerial view of North Coates airfield from directly overhead, in late 1943 or 1944, showing the new concrete east-west runway; close examination will reveal 35 Beaufighters dispersed around the airfield. (Photo: Crown Copyright, via Brian Stafford)

A camp cinema was constructed that also served as a theatre, where the Christmas pantomime and other productions were staged. This was where a young Max Bygraves, a mechanic in the Motor Transport Section, presented his monthly revue 'Chocks Away'. There was a football field used by all ranks, that doubled as the cricket pitch during the summer.

In addition to the wooden billets constructed earlier, in 1943 a number of brick structures were built, including some married quarters, and terraced accommodation for WAAF personnel. These were near the guard room at the main entrance, close to where the parade ground was already located. A nearby 'astrodome' type building was built for simulated gunnery training.

The war-time Control Tower at North Coates; constructed by a local builder in the 1930's, it was unusual in being made of timber; in use throughout the war, it was damaged by fire in the 1980's and subsequently demolished. (Photo: Crown Copyright, via Brian Stafford)

Life at the Camp – Spartan but Happy

RAF North Coates was not a comfortable 'home-from-home'. Conditions during the winter were bleak. An easterly or northerly wind blowing off the North Sea through the open airfield would pile drifts of snow up against the walls, and sometimes under the doors and into the buildings themselves.

The relatively spartan conditions aside, the recollections of those who served there suggest that, by and large, the atmosphere was a happy one. Empathetic station commanders and squadron COs were remembered, especially during the Strike Wing years of 1942–45. By the middle years of the war the divide between officers and other ranks that characterised pre-war British society had at least blurred. There was a significant proportion of Dominion and other non-British officers and NCOs amongst the station's 1,500 or so personnel, which included around 200 WAAFs, and this injected more social informality.

The book *Home Sweet Home* is a collection of letters to his mother written by F/Sgt. Bob Kimberley, a scholarship boy who became a commercial artist before joining the wartime RAF in June 1941 and serving as a Flight Sergeant pilot on 236 Squadron at North Coates in 1944. He writes about his training in the UK and Canada and, briefly, about his days at North Coates. His poignant letters about his day-to-day life reveal the loneliness and confusion of a young man doing his duty. There is none of the 'Boys Own' bravura that can often be portrayed as typical of Second World War pilots, and it is certain that Kimberley's letters reflect much more closely the everyday preoccupations of most of the inhabitants of the huts and mess-halls at North Coates. In his short career Bob Kimberley was one of the many who 'did what he was told to do', routinely displaying the courage to fly on dangerous missions, on the basis that 'it probably won't happen to me'. However, it did happen to him, and he and his navigator, F/Sgt. Macnee, were shot down and killed on 10 September 1944 on a Strike off Den Helder. He had been married for just six months, and the day before had written to his mother that *very soon now it seems that this damn war will be over and that'll be our biggest worries and fears gone. So hold on a little longer, Mum, and we'll make things worthwhile once again.*

Life on the base was rarely interrupted by enemy attacks during the Strike Wing period. There were eleven 'hit-and-run' attacks during the war, but most were in 1940–41, including one random raid by a lone Ju88 in November 1941, when the attacker was hit by the camp's RAF Regiment anti-aircraft gunners and brought down. The raids did little real damage and caused no serious injuries.

Some excitement was provided in April 1943 when two aircraftmen, named Robinson and Walton, *unlawfully stole* one of 143 Squadron's newly delivered Beaufighters, according to the squadron ORB, and *attempted to fly to Eire*. Both men had escaped from the guardroom on the previous day, where they were awaiting Court Martial for stealing. They crashed when attempting to take off and were re-apprehended. At the subsequent Court Martial they were both jailed for eighteen months.

Unquestionably there was what would now be called a 'drinking culture' on the station, and it is easy to understand why. The camp messes and the pubs off-base offered a refuge from the stress and fear of combat flying, and for those working on the ground these provided a break from the pressure, rigour and tedium of their work. Opportunities for a break from camp were welcomed and Grimsby, with its pubs, dance halls, cinemas and ice rink, was accessible by bus or camp transport, and generally remembered with affection.

There were also close operational links between Grimsby and North Coates. The 'GY' trawlers were a familiar sight to the aircraft flying overhead. The air-sea rescue launches based at Grimsby docks were under the direction of RAF North Coates and saved the lives of many ditched

A celebratory evening in the officers' mess in 1945; the 254 Squadron commander, W/Cdr. Dave Cartridge, is sitting in the centre with the tankard. (Photo: Vimpany archive)

Concert at North Coates in May 1945; stage shows were an essential ingredient of life on a wartime RAF station, and many performances involved station personnel, although this one was probably by a professional theatre company. (Photo: Vimpany archive)

airmen. One of the most dramatic rescues from a ditched Beaufighter was due to the heroic efforts of the Grimsby trawler *Median* on 20 July 1944. A catastrophic engine failure while flying on a Wing reconnaissance caused a Beaufighter of 254 squadron piloted by Canadian F/Lt. Tony Adams to plunge into the sea off Flamborough Head at 320 mph. This was observed by the *Median,* which made straight for the crash site. The aircraft sank immediately, and Adams was never found and presumed killed. However his navigator, F/O Arthur Steel, although badly injured, managed to release himself from the sinking aircraft and was spotted on the surface by the *Median's* crew. One of the crewmen, James Daykin, dived overboard and rescued Steel. For this life-saving feat both Daykin and *Median's* Skipper Rogers were decorated.

A WAAF Remembers

Sylvia Darby, a WAAF at North Coates in 1942-43; she recalled the daily life of the station, and also the sadness when crews failed to return, as well as the camaraderie. (Photo: Darby family)

A personal memoir written by Sylvia Darby, a WAAF stationed at North Coates for two years during 1942–43, paints a vivid picture of typical daily life for the many ground personnel of the time.[1] She supervised the Clothing Stores and struggled to prevent frequent attempts by some personnel to 'fiddle' the stores and issues system. She gives a poignant description of her most distressing task, sorting through the belongings of aircrew who had lost their lives, before returning their possessions to their families. Sylvia also recounts talking with aircrew as they ate a 'special' meal before taking off on night missions and recalls that the prospect of these clearly frightened them.

Another frightening and upsetting incident occurred when a Beaufighter preparing for take-off suffered an engine failure and, out of control, collided into a hanger, causing a huge fuel fire and much damage. Fortunately, the crew escaped and a potential huge ammunition explosion was narrowly avoided, but many onlookers were fearful that '*the whole camp would be blown up*.' A sad fatality witnessed by Sylvia was that of a horse badly burnt in the blaze.

Sylvia recalls plenty of lighter moments, and trips into Grimsby were enjoyable. The ice rink was a popular place to meet the boys, as were trips to the cinema and a meal of egg and chips or tea at the 'Toc H'. (These were rest and recreation centres for all ranks, run by a Christian charity, founded during the First World War.) There was regular entertainment on the Station itself. As

1   Darby archive.

106

WAAF team photo, 1943; there were around 200 WAAFs stationed at North Coates; a smiling Sylvia Darby is eighth from the right in the third row. (Photo: Crown Copyright via Darby family)

with many established bases, North Coates had its own cinema and theatre hall. Western films were popular at the time and theatre productions included home-grown revues, as well as visits from ENSA and professional theatre groups such as the famous Donald Wolfit Shakespeare Company. Concerts ranged from classical recitals to dance band music, and Sylvia remembers that all the service bands were very good, as most of the musicians had been in top London dance bands before they enlisted.

On one occasion a station night defence exercise entailed the WAAFs defending the camp against the infantrymen of the Green Howards Regiment. It was all over quickly, perhaps because many of the WAAFs allowed themselves to be captured …

Distinguished Visitors

27 May 1943 was memorable for a visit by King George VI and Queen Elizabeth, who were greeted by a formal parade. The King and Queen inspected the squadrons, spoke to aircrews and toured the aircraft hangers with the Station Commander, Group Captain 'Giles' Gilson. The King had been following progress on the introduction of rocket projectiles and, viewing from the sea wall, was given a live demonstration of the new weapon by W/Cdr. Wheeler, who 'attacked' a target on the beach. This must have been an impressive display because many years later a Strike Wing veteran met Queen Elizabeth, now the Queen Mother, and mentioned that he had been present during her visit to North Coates. She immediately recalled seeing the rockets and how they had impressed the King.[2]

A few days after the Royal visit, the Secretary of State for Air, Sir Archibald Sinclair, made a visit. His parade ground speech apparently included the words of exhortation *I promise you blood!* which did not have quite the effect intended on Dick Vimpany and the other aircrew present.[3]

---

2   Nesbit, *The Strike Wings*, p.74
3   Vimpany archive.

Royal visitors inspect a Beaufighter; station CO Group Captain Gilson checks his watch as the King and Queen leave the hangar to watch W/Cdr. Wheeler's rocket attack demonstration on the station foreshore. (Photo: Crown Copyright via Darby family)

The Royal motorcade leaving RAF North Coates in May 1943, with station personnel lining the route and cheering the King and Queen's car. The row of hangars is to the left of the road. (Photo: Crown Copyright/Air Historical Branch)

RAF Donna Nook – North Coates' satellite station

Donna Nook airfield was located two miles south of North Coates, adjacent to foreshore acquired by the RAF after the First World War for use as a practice bombing range. At the outbreak of the war in 1939 Donna Nook became a decoy airfield, complete with inflatable dummy Blenheim aircraft that were sufficiently convincing that on one occasion the site attracted an enemy bombing raid.

Winston Churchill visited Donna Nook when inspecting coastal defence installations. Already useful as an emergency landing ground for damaged aircraft, at the end of 1940 it was brought under Coastal Command control as a satellite of North Coates, to serve as a relief airfield. Its two grass runways were upgraded, and its support buildings extended. At the end of 1941 around one hundred personnel were based at Donna Nook, mostly billeted in temporary huts.

In 1941 Donna Nook was also the home the Canadian 407 Squadron, flying Lockheed Hudsons on anti-shipping missions. They fought a brave and distinguished campaign from Donna Nook and were known as the 'Demon' squadron for their exploits. In early 1943 Donna Nook became a

Aerial view of Donna Nook airfield; barely distinguishable, the north-south grass runway and east-west grass runway are top-centre of the photograph. (Photo: Crown Copyright, Vimpany archive)

temporary airfield for the North Coates Strike Wing itself while the concrete runway was being laid at North Coates. By late 1944 however, Donna Nook's operational use was scaled down significantly, as the North Coates Strike Wing was reduced to two squadrons and their successful campaign over the North Sea shipping lanes was largely over. Nevertheless, it remained a welcome landfall for stricken or lost aircraft until VE Day.

In peacetime Donna Nook was used as a prisoner of war camp (some POW accommodation blocks are still in use as farm buildings today) and then as a maintenance unit depot, until the RAF returned in 1973 to operate the foreshore as a NATO weapons range. This remains active today, with the bombing exercises publicised locally and often attracting small crowds of onlookers. Inevitably, from the Strike Wing era, very little remains of the former airfield, which has reverted to farmland.

8

Balance Sheet

The men who served in the North Coates Strike Wing entertained few doubts about the role they had played, the success they had achieved, and the price they had paid. In a letter written in 1995 Dick Vimpany judged that '*Although losses of aircraft were high … it became clear that before the end of 1944 the Germans could not safely use the sea lanes and our losses were justified.*'[1]

In a paper published in Aerospace magazine in 1979,[2] Paddy Burns listed three objectives which the North Coates Strike Wing had sought to achieve :

- To sink ships.
- To compel the Germans to sacrifice the convenience of Rotterdam, with its excellent port facilities and communications with the Ruhr.
- To strengthen the reluctance of Swedish crews to sail their ships beyond Emden.

He went on to discuss how each of these objectives had been met. The Wing had suffered significant losses over the two years that it operated, with 241 aircrew killed, but it had succeeded in what it was deployed to do, and against a brave and determined adversary.

Other writers have since analysed the 'balance sheet' of the anti-shipping campaign in more detail, and at several levels. The first of these assesses the impact of the Strike Wings on German shipping. This analysis is relatively straightforward and its conclusions clear - the Wings successfully achieved what they set out to do.

The second question asked, much wider in scope, is about the impact of the anti-shipping campaign on the outcome of the war. Did the Strike Wings, including North Coates, make a real difference in reducing the supply of material vital to the German war effort; or were they a sideshow, fighting and winning their fierce local battles, but having no significant strategic impact on Germany's ability to continue to fight the war? The conclusions here are more nuanced.

---

1   Vimpany archive - unpublished
2   Burns '*Anti-Shipping Strikes 1939–45*' Aerospace Magazine, 1979

This debate also gives rise to intriguing 'what if ?' questions. Specifically, what if more resources had been devoted to the Strike Wings, and at an earlier stage of the war, diverting even a small part of Britain's war effort away from the massive bombing campaign that dominated the country's offensive strategy? That discussion is more divisive and there can never be a definitive conclusion.

Collecting the evidence

At the end of the war a huge amount of time and effort went into research and analysis of the impact of the strategic bombing campaign undertaken against Germany, and the British Bombing Survey Unit (BBSU) produced a comprehensive report on the bombing campaign and its impact. This was understandable, as Britain's strategic bombing effort had absorbed a huge share of the nation's resources: more than 10,000 heavy bombers were manufactured during the war and fifty-five thousand men were killed, almost one in seven of all British deaths in action, with another ten thousand men taken prisoner.

Perhaps unsurprisingly, no similar survey was carried out for Coastal Command's much smaller scale anti-shipping campaign. Various reports did appear, but these all lacked much of the detailed research and analysis seen in the BBSU's work on the bombing campaign, and it was not until 1947 that a full assessment of the anti-shipping campaign was compiled.

That work was undertaken by the Senior Naval Officer attached to Coastal Command for much of the war, Captain D.V. Peyton-Ward CBE. He used a wide variety of sources, including German records that had become available, to compile a detailed list of German-controlled shipping sunk or damaged in north-west Europe between mid-1940 and the end of the war. This report was submitted to the Air Historical Branch and, with some small amendments made later, is the definitive data source for the anti-shipping campaign.

Strike Wing Impact on Shipping

Peyton-Ward identified a total of 365 vessels sunk and 145 damaged by aircraft controlled by Coastal Command between April 1940 and May 1945. These ships included naval escorts and harbour defence vessels as well as merchantmen. There is some question about the definition of 'damaged' shipping that he used, as his numbers do not always tally with what was reported by the squadrons at the time, and it is likely that the number of German ships suffering some damage from air attack was higher than the final number established by Peyton-Ward.

One additional sinking and some other damaged vessels that Peyton-Ward's team had omitted were identified later by Christina Goulter, so that the final numbers are now recognised as being 366 ships sunk and 145 damaged.[3] These figures were achieved for the loss of 857 Coastal Command aircraft.

---

3   Goulter, *A Forgotten Offensive*, p.274

By comparison, a total of 638 German-controlled ships were sunk by mines during the same period, for the loss of 450 aircraft (42 of which were from Coastal Command and 408 from Bomber Command).[4] Taken across the whole war, therefore, minelaying was clearly a far more cost-effective anti-shipping strategy.

Anti-Shipping Offensive : April 1940 to May 1945	Ships sunk	Aircraft lost	Aircraft lost per ship sunk
Mines (Bomber & Coastal Commands)	638	450	0.71
Air Attack (Coastal Command)	366	857	2.34

Source: *From Goulter*, p. 297 & p.353.

It is necessary however to distinguish between the three-year period leading up to early 1943, and the subsequent two years, after the launch of the Strike Wing offensive. The first period was characterised by poor strategy and tactics and inadequate resources, resulting in very high losses of aircraft and aircrew for every ship sunk. From April 1943 onwards, the Strike Wing era, the number of ships sunk and damaged increased markedly, and this was accompanied by a significant fall in the number of aircraft and crews lost.

Working from operational records, Nesbit listed a total of 215 vessels that had been sunk by all of the Strike Wing squadrons, nine of these in total, after the formation of the first Wing at North Coates in late 1942.[5] A further 59 merchant ships were seriously damaged (he does not estimate the number of escorts that were damaged). The total tonnage sunk was just over 300,000, which he judged to be around two-thirds of all German tonnage sunk by aircraft during this two-and-a-half-year period. As well as merchantmen and surface warships, these Strike Wing sinkings included eleven U-boats, nine of them in the last month of the war, and a number of midget submarines, also towards the end of the war. *(See Appendix III.)*

Nesbit estimates that the Strike Wings' total tally of ships sunk was achieved at the cost of 250 aircraft lost to enemy action. Extracting these numbers for Strike Wing ship sinkings and aircraft losses from Goulter's totals for all of Coastal Command after April 1940, the effectiveness of the Strike Wings is very clear - they accounted for well over half of all German ships sunk by aircraft attack, but less than a third of all the aircraft lost to enemy action.

The contrast between the results for the Strike Wings and other forms of air attack is striking.

Anti-Shipping Offensive : April 1940 to May 1945	Ships sunk	Aircraft lost	Aircraft lost per ship sunk
All Air Attacks (Coastal Command)	366	857	2.34
Of which :			
Strike Wings, Nov 1942-May 1945	215	250	1.16
All other Air Attacks	151	607	4.02

Source: Derived from: *Goulter*, p.353; *Nesbit*, p.24; *Nesbit Appendix III.*

---

4   Goulter, *A Forgotten Offensive*, p.297
5   Nesbit, *The Strike Wings*, Appendix III

North Coates Strike Wing Results

The North Coates Wing comprised 236 and 254 Squadrons from October 1942 until May 1945, with 143 Squadron also forming part of the Wing from January 1943 until October 1944. A total of 125 ships were sunk by these three squadrons during the time when they part of the Wing, with a total tonnage of 145,890.[6] This includes ships sunk by squadrons on detachment away from North Coates, or when operating with other squadrons that were not part of the North Coates Wing. These sinkings represent around half of all the German shipping sunk by the Strike Wings in total.

If the U-boats and midget submarines sunk during the closing weeks of the war are excluded, the total number of ships sunk by the North Coates Wing was 103, with a total tonnage of 142,049 (see Appendix IV). These 103 surface ships comprised 25 merchant vessels, with a total tonnage of 79,238 tons (average tonnage of 3,170), and 78 surface warships. The latter included minesweepers and flak ships, Sperrbrechers, harbour defence vessels and E-boats.

The Strike Wing Memorial at Cleethorpes remembers 120 aircraft lost and 241 aircrew killed while flying with one of the three Strike Wing squadrons (their names are listed on the Roll of Honour in Cleethorpes Town Hall). This equates to the loss of 1.16 aircraft for each surface ship sunk. The figure is 1.0 aircraft lost per ship sunk if the U-boats and midget submarines destroyed during the last months of the war are included. These results are in line with those of the Strike Wing force as a whole.

The pattern of sinkings by the North Coates Wing reflects the unfolding of the campaign. From April 1943 it fought a series of actions at Wing strength against large, heavily defended convoys making their way along the Dutch coast to and from Rotterdam, sinking merchant ships at an average rate of more than one per month. By the summer of 1944, however, the success of the Strike Wings had severely restricted the ability of German convoys to sail during daylight hours. With fewer opportunities to attack convoys and large merchantmen, in the late summer of 1944 aircraft from North Coates roamed further up and down the coast of Holland and France, often in the company of squadrons from other Wings, and destroyed a significant number of minesweepers and harbour protection vessels - but no merchantmen (see Appendix IV).

After a barren period through the winter of 1944–45, due to a lack of potential targets in its area, the North Coates Wing ended the war operating for 24 hours from Helmond in the Netherlands, from where it launched its 'rampages' down the Kattegat and through the Great Belt into the Baltic. On its last two sorties of the war the Wing sank ten ships, including three merchantmen and a tanker, as well as five U-boats and a minesweeper.

---

6   Nesbit, *The Strike Wings*, Appendix III

A job well done

There can be no doubt that the North Coates Strike Wing won its war. It had accomplished its mission by the late summer of 1944, when heavy losses of merchantmen and naval escorts had compelled the Germans to abandon Rotterdam as the major route for raw materials into the Ruhr. Thereafter the Wing's job was to maintain the pressure on the enemy, pinning the Germans down in their heavily defended ports, before participating in the final offensive to destroy Germany's maritime presence. When the end of the war eventually came, everyone who served at North Coates could be very proud of the success they had achieved. There could be no doubt - they had *'forced the enemy off the sea'*.

The Wider Impact

The second question posed earlier is whether the success of the Strike Wings had any significant impact on the outcome of wider war in Europe. There are two areas to address. The first is the direct impact of the Strike Wing operations on the German industries being supplied by the ships that the Wing was attacking and sinking. The second is the extent to which the activities of the Strike Wing diverted resources away from other, strategically important theatres.

On German industry

Post-war analysis of German shipping data showed that from the spring of 1943 onwards there was a steep decline in the volume of shipping and freight handled by the port of Rotterdam. In May 1942, an average of 106,000 tons of shipping was using Rotterdam every day, compared to just 37,000 at Emden. One year later, after just three successful Strike Wing attacks on convoys on their way to or from Rotterdam, the positions were reversed, with Rotterdam handling just 37,000 tons of shipping per day and Emden now handling 100,000 tons.[7]

This was partly influenced by the decision of the Swedish government in May 1943 to stop underwriting the insurance of Swedish merchant ships operating south of Emden. Although only one Swedish ship had been sunk by the North Coates Wing during its first convoy Strikes (the *Narvik* of 4,251 tons, on 29 April) the effectiveness of the RAF's new anti-shipping offensive had clearly raised the risk of losses to an unacceptable level.

As the Strike Wing campaign continued through 1944 there was a noticeable decrease in the volume of trade between Germany and the Scandinavian countries. Germany's total volume of iron ore imports from Sweden and Norway during the first half of 1944 was around one third of the volume imported for the whole of 1943,[8] implying a fall of at least 30% on a like-for-like basis. It is difficult to isolate the direct impact of the reduction in

---

7   Slessor Dispatch
8   Goulter, *A Forgotten Offensive*, p.354 Table 4

Rotterdam shipping traffic shipping on trade volumes overall and industrial production. However, Goulter estimates that Coastal Command's anti-shipping campaign was responsible for a 10% fall in German steel production between January 1944 and March 1945,[9] and it seems reasonable to assume that the North Coates Strike Wing played a significant part in this outcome.

However, neither the increasing difficulties of getting shipping into Rotterdam, nor the fall in the volume of Germany's iron ore imports, made a significant dent in its production of armaments. The fact was that German armaments production continued to increase right through until late 1944. It was not until September 1944, three months after the Allies had returned to mainland Europe and were starting to push towards the Ruhr, that there was a noticeable fall in Germany's production of crude steel.[10] Germany manufactured more aircraft, tanks and heavy field guns in 1944 than it had done in 1940, 1941 and 1942 combined.[11] It was only during the last few months of the war, with the allies pressing into Germany itself from both east and west, that German industrial output collapsed.

This was an extraordinary achievement by German industry, and a major surprise after the war to the allied leadership, which had consistently underestimated the capacity and resilience of the German economy and its manufacturing capability. There has been much analysis and debate about Germany's ability to maintain its armaments production, including the impact of the leadership and organisation skills of Albert Speer and his colleagues after 1942, and the availability of almost unlimited forced labour from the occupied territories. As well as these factors, most historians now agree that Germany had entered the war with its economy operating well below its full potential, and not on anything like a total war footing. There was substantial surplus capacity, that could be mobilised properly, which Speer did.

The area of most interest to British historians, however, has been the failure of Britain's strategic bombing campaign to destroy Germany's industrial capacity, or displace or deter its labour force. Bomber Command absorbed the lion's share of Britain's resources, and it flattened many German cities and killed or made homeless hundreds of thousands of their inhabitants, but Germany's armaments production continued almost unabated until the last six months of the war.

It is in that context that the wider impact of the Strike Wings, including North Coates, must be judged. For the loss of 250 aircraft, 120 of these flying from North Coates, the Strike Wings choked off an important German supply route. That was not enough to materially affect German armaments production. However, nor was a massive three-year bombing campaign that cost 8,300 aircraft and 55,000 aircrew. And nor did any Strike Wing pilot or navigator have to experience any disquiet, then or later, about the civilian

9   Goulter, *Royal Air Force Historical Society Journal*, Issue 33, 2005, p.37.
10   Goulter, *A Forgotten Offensive*, p.355 Table 6
11   Max Hastings, *Bomber Command* (London, Michael Joseph, 1979) Appendix D, p.370

deaths they were causing. As Roy Nesbit remarked, '*In so far as any conflict can be 'clean', this was the war fought by the Strike Wings*'.[12]

Diverting resources from other fronts

Historians and commentators have concluded that the Strike Wings did cause a very substantial diversion of German men and guns away from other theatres of the war.[13] Defending against air attack required anti-aircraft guns on German ships, manned by trained gunners. There were also shore batteries and port defences needed to keep the Strike Wings at bay. The whole German defensive effort consisted of thousands of guns, including 150mm and the highly effective 88mm, as well as 50mm and 20mm weapons, and many thousands of trained men.

This diversion of resources was important before D-Day, when Germany was resisting the advance of the Russians on the eastern front. It was equally important after the opening of the second front in June 1944. Throughout the period when the Strike Wings were operating, the German men and guns that had to be used to defend its shipping in the North Sea would have formed a valuable addition to their armies, as these strove to hold back the numerically superior allies on both the eastern and western fronts. Within the context of the war as a whole, and whatever its other results, the anti-shipping campaign should therefore be seen as a successful and important complementary action, supporting the strategically vital areas of the conflict that delivered the Allied victory.

A final question: 'What if … ?'

An intriguing question alluded to earlier was whether a greater commitment of Britain's resources to anti-shipping operations could have resulted in a different outcome. Specifically, what might have happened if there had been fewer Lancasters built and dispatched to bomb Germany from 1942 onwards, and more Beaufighters built and dispatched in Strike Wings to attack German ships in the North Sea? Could the war have ended sooner, with less loss of life? Two writers about the anti-shipping campaign both address this issue, and they draw different conclusions.

On the one hand, Goulter concluded that a large-scale diversion of resources from Bomber Command to Coastal Command would have had a potentially negative impact on Britain's war effort overall. Although many of Bomber Command's targets were *less than vital* to German industrial production,[14] many of them were, in particular around oil installations and transport infrastructure. A significantly smaller bomber force would have jeopardised their ability to hit these important targets. At the same time, by mid-1944 much less German shipping was moving south of Emden, leaving fewer targets for the North Coates Strike Wing to attack. Additional aircraft

---

12   Nesbit, *The Strike Wings*, p.252
13   Goulter, *A Forgotten Offensive*, p.317
14   Goulter, *A Forgotten Offensive*, p.317

and crews would not have made any difference, and indeed several squadrons were transferred out of 16 Group and moved north to 18 Group, to operate along the coast of Norway.

Nesbit, on the other hand, argued that it would have been *far more advantageous for the Allied war effort if resources had been diverted from Bomber Command to Coastal Command*.[15] This conclusion was based mainly on manpower 'gain factor' analysis carried out by the BBSU. This calculated that a Strike Wing Beaufighter gained a manpower benefit in terms of the losses it inflicted of around three times the manpower cost that it incurred. The equivalent calculation for a four-engine bomber was a gain of one-for-one at best, with an eminent wartime scientist writing that *the actual effort in manpower and resources that was expended in bombing Germany was greater than the value in manpower of the damage caused*.[16]

Both of these viewpoints can be supported, but both can also be challenged. In particular, the question of strategic priorities and resource allocation needs to address the different phases of both the anti-shipping campaign and the bombing campaign.

It is clear that from early 1944 onwards Allied bombers were successfully targeting oil installations and transport infrastructure, and that the Strike Wings had already achieved a dominance along the Dutch coast. However, there are two other important factors to consider. First, before 1944, oil and transport targets were a lower priority for Bomber Command - their attacks were directed against industrial cities. Secondly, the successful campaign against the German oil installations was mainly undertaken by the US air force, not by the RAF. As the German General in charge of aircraft production commented after the war *the British inflicted grievous and bloody injuries upon us ... but the Americans stabbed us in the heart*.[17] It is therefore difficult to argue that a reduction in RAF Bomber Command resources would have led to less effective raids on oil and transport targets; and certainly not in 1942 or 1943.

On the other hand, the main problem with broad-brush assertions about 'gain factor' is that statistical analysis based on manpower calculations is a very blunt instrument. For example, it does not differentiate between high-value targets and less important ones, and it does not consider the different strategic situations prevailing at different phases of both the Strike Wing and bombing campaigns. It is difficult to argue, for example, that fewer Lancasters and more Beaufighters and Mosquitoes in 1944 would have altered the course of the war.

It can be argued, however, that more Beaufighter Strike Wings, operating from mid-1942, could potentially have had a greater impact on German armaments production than was achieved by Bomber Command in 1942 and 1943. This is because in early 1942 Germany suffered a serious merchant shipping crisis, and this could have been exploited to put massive pressure on all of Germany's supply lines.

---

15   Nesbit, *The Strike Wings*, p.250
16   Sir Henry Tizzard quoted in Nesbit, *The Strike Wings*, p.249.
17   Hastings, *Bomber Command*, p.350

Before 1942, although poorly managed, the capacity of the German-controlled merchant fleet was adequate to meet demand, and fairly stable. Losses due to mines and aircraft attack were balanced by new capacity being built, damaged ships repaired, and the addition to the fleet of ships captured and requisitioned in occupied territories. In early 1942, however, German shipping capacity had become very stretched. The main reason was the transfer of a significant proportion of the merchant fleet to serve the German military, principally to carry men and supplies in the Baltic. At the same time the Kriegsmarine conscripted many experienced merchant seamen into naval vessels. The effect of these actions was exacerbated by the exceptionally harsh winter in the Baltic, the steady success of the British mine-laying campaign, and slower working in the shipyards in occupied countries, delaying both damage repairs and new ship construction.

When it became clear to the Germans that there was now a serious lack of merchant shipping capacity, which would have potentially serious consequences for the supply of raw materials, a powerful new organisation was created to rectify the situation. The appointment of Kaufman to oversee the management of Germany's merchant shipping capacity mirrored Hitler's appointment of Speer to get German industry onto a proper war footing. Like Speer, Kaufman reported directly to Hitler, and used his wide-ranging powers to implement numerous new initiatives, successfully restoring Germany's merchant shipping capacity through the course of 1942 and early 1943.

Britain's leadership knew this, because the Ministry of Economic Warfare had correctly identified the Germans' problems in early 1942, as well as their subsequent efforts to restore the situation. However, by this time the bombing campaign had become strategic dogma for Britain's war leaders, and there was simply no willingness or ability to consider any different ways to attack Germany. Its industrial cities were going to be bombed, using a vast number of men and machines, and that was that. Britain's resources were therefore geared to deliver the Lancasters and crews needed to do that.

A strong case can be made that if MEW's information had been correctly evaluated and had led to a decision to create and deploy Strike Wings sooner, and in larger numbers, the weakness in the German merchant shipping fleet could have been better exploited. If the successful North Coates Strikes of April 1943 onwards had been delivered from the summer of 1942 onwards, it is likely that the German merchant fleet would not have recovered as successfully as it did. As a result, there would simply have been too few ships available to meet all of Germany's needs. That in turn would have had a much more significant impact on Germany's raw materials supply lines, and a likely knock-on effect on armaments production.

Hindsight is a wonderful thing, but it is difficult not to speculate that if more men and machines had been committed to a Strike Wing campaign just nine months earlier, they would have enjoyed even more success, and could have played a central role in bringing the war in Europe to an end before May 1945, with fewer lives lost.

Postscript

Job Done – A sudden end for the Wing

Following their final 'rampage' through the Kattegat in the closing days of hostilities in Europe, 236 and 254 Squadrons returned to their home base at North Coates on 4 May. The next day, at Luneburg Heath, Field Marshall Montgomery accepted the surrender of all German forces in north-west Europe, including naval forces. The general surrender came into effect on 7 May, and next day the RAF North Coates Commander ordered an 08:00 parade for all ranks and announced news of the cessation of the war in Europe. A drumhead service was followed by a day of football and cricket and an evening dance. All ranks were stood down for 24 hours, followed by leave for some and celebrations in Grimsby and the surrounding area for others.

Although suddenly no longer required in Europe, rumours circulated that the Wing could soon be needed for the war in Asia, still at its height. But on 25 May, a visit to the station from the Air Officer Commanding 16 Group, Air Vice Marshall Hopps, brought the announcement that 236 Squadron was disbanded *with immediate effect*. Within a few short weeks its aircrews, groundcrews and aircraft were dispersed to other units. The end of the war found 143 Squadron in Scotland, from where it was now flying Mosquitoes as part of the Banff Strike Wing. This squadron too was disbanded on 25 May.

The future of 254 Squadron was uncertain, although it remained operational and continued training activities at North Coates until it was ordered to move to RAF Chivenor in Devon at the end of June, and subsequently to RAF Thorney Island on the Sussex coast. It remained available with its Beaufighters to take part in the war against Japan if required, but Japan capitulated in mid-August. In 1946, 254 Squadron was re-numbered 42 Squadron, Coastal Command, but its torpedo bombing capability was discontinued.

Post-war Roles for a Frontline Base

For several years after the War, RAF North Coates, the once lively station and self-contained war-time community of well over a thousand souls, was put to a number of peacetime uses by the RAF. First it served as a facility for various training, maintenance and ordnance disposal units that were scrapping wrecked and surplus aircraft. The buildings that comprised the base, now generally in poor condition, were subjected to several winters of foul weather, including the great East Coast Flood of 1953 that badly affected the entire camp and airfield. Clearly, the remote and exposed location was not suited to peacetime training needs. The station remained open, but only on a care and maintenance basis, until the mid-1950s, when a unit of two Sycamore helicopters arrived to provide an experimental search and rescue service. These distinctive yellow machines, curious at the time, became a familiar sight in the Lincolnshire skies.

Frontline duty again – the Bloodhound era

The departure of the helicopters in late 1956 coincided with preparations for a serious new role for North Coates. It was to assume a place on the new front line of Britain's defence system, this time in the Cold War. In 1957 modernisation of the station began, including the construction of forty-eight missile pads and the installation of the associated extensive cabling and electronics. The uninitiated observer would not have realised that behind the Second World War exterior of Hangar 5 was housed the state-of-the-art Tactical Control Centre for the Bloodhound Surface-to-Air Missile (SAM) system. There followed a period of experiment and testing for the Bloodhound Mark 1 and later the Mark 2.

In 1960 the station became the headquarters of 148 Wing, of which 264 Guided Missile Squadron was based at North Coates, and the base living accommodation was extensively modernised. As part of NATO, these units' role was to counter the Soviet nuclear threat from the air with the Bloodhound SAMs. When the improved Mark 2 Bloodhound was introduced in October 1963, 25 Squadron was re-formed to work up and operate these.

The initial Bloodhound phase at North Coates ended in 1971 when the missiles were re-deployed to Germany. The station then remained mothballed until 1976, when it re-opened as the base for 'B' Flight of 85 Squadron, equipped with twenty-four Mark 2 Bloodhounds. In late 1980's the station also accommodated the Bloodhound Missile System Training School.

Civilian Life

Fortunately, during their thirty years of deployment the Bloodhound SAMs were not called upon to intercept an attack by the Soviet Air Force and in 1990, after sixty-five years of military use, North Coates was shut down as a missile and military base. Its personnel were posted elsewhere, its weaponry re-deployed and, unsentimentally, the real estate transferred to the Defence Land Agency for commercial disposal.

The total site comprising airfield, technical area and former married quarters, was acquired by a property company and over the next ten years was the subject of various proposals to locate aviation heritage projects and

Schoolfriends-in-arms, 45 years on. 254 Squadron navigators Freddy Hinks and Dick Vimpany in front of Bloodhound surface-to-air missiles at RAF North Coates, during the Strike Wing reunion in October 1988. (Photo: Vimpany archive)

Strike Wing veterans meet Cold War warriors; briefing in the North Coates missile control room, October 1988. R to L: George Cox. (254), Dick Vimpany. (254), Pat Fry. (236), Tom Neilson. (254) with explanations from S/Ldr Stevenson. (Photo: Vimpany archive)

commercial aviation services, using the airfield and remaining hangers. Enthusiasm grew for a local private flying club, and the present North Coates Flying Club was set up on a sound basis in 1995, with arrangements to use Hangar 4 and the runway. The Technical Site and its relatively modern buildings were acquired by a US-based Christian missionary organisation for use as a training institute.

Further property transactions from 1999 onwards resulted in a satisfactory arrangement whereby the flying area of the Airfield, including Hanger 4, was transferred to Kilmaurs Holdings Ltd. Its directors are enthusiastically supportive of private flying and the heritage of the site and allow the Flying Club to continue to use and operate the present flying area. The provision by the Club of a grass runway alongside the track of the former concrete runway means that the Club's activities can continue, preserving the tradition of active flying at North Coates, and its proud aviation heritage

North Coates Flying Club

Established in 1995, the thriving Flying Club keeps aviation alive at North Coates, as is clear from the many and varied aircraft based at the airfield. Several well-attended flying meetings are held each year and the Club provides a social and leisure base for active pilots and non-flying members.

The Club is keenly aware of the history of the airfield and has become the de-facto custodian of its aviation heritage. It presently holds a collection of some four hundred photo images, archive film, and a growing collection of memorabilia and artefacts, including a rare example of a Bloodhound Mark 1 guided missile. Within the historic No. 4 Hangar that the Club occupies there is an exhibition commemorating the history of military aviation at North Coates.

North Coates airfield today, with pre-war Hangar 4 in the background; the aviation heritage is today in the safe hands of the North Coates Flying Club and airfield owners. (Photo: John Tuck)

The Veterans Return

In 1988, shortly before the closure of their old base, a gathering of surviving members of the Strike Wing aircrews was held the station, as part of the annual reunion of members of the North Coates Strike Wing Association. Evening dinner reunions had taken place each year since the late 1940s, normally held in the London area for convenience. But in 1988 the event was an opportunity for the former crews, by then in their late sixties and seventies, to get together for a day at their old base. One of them was heard to say that *'it hadn't changed much'*[1]. But it had. With few of the Second World War structures remaining, there were now buildings from the 1960s standing on the footprints of earlier timber structures; but the veteran's comment reflected that the layout and atmosphere of a typical RAF station had survived.

The Reunion Dinner in 1988 was held in Grimsby and chaired by their former Wing Leader 'Nebbie' Wheeler, who had retired from the RAF as Air Chief Marshall Sir Neil Wheeler. Reunions were convivial and were supported by the frequent and popular participation of another Wing Leader, Tony Gadd.

All three Strike Wing squadrons were well represented at their reunion in October 1988; many of the veterans visited their wartime base, including W/Cdr. Tony Gadd, seated eighth from right, and Dick Vimpany and Freddie Gardiner, seated fifth and sixth from the right respectively. (Photo: Vimpany archive)

'Failed to Return' – the Fallen

The last significant gathering of the remaining men of the North Coates Strike Wing Association was in September 1999 for the unveiling of the memorial they had funded for their comrades who were killed, mainly in the battles over the North Sea between 1943–45. Unveiled by Sir Neil Wheeler, the stunning bronze statue, positioned on High Cliff, Cleethorpes, is of a Strike Wing airman in flying kit scanning the North Sea. It honours the 241 men of the North Coates squadrons who gave their lives on active service with the Wing, and especially those who have no known grave.

In late 2021 the memorial was restored by the local RAF Association and re-dedicated on 5 December in a ceremony on High Cliff hosted by the

---

1   Vimpany archive.

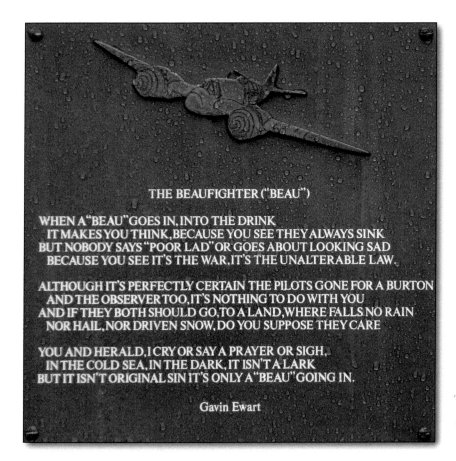

THE BEAUFIGHTER ("BEAU")

WHEN A "BEAU" GOES IN, INTO THE DRINK
IT MAKES YOU THINK, BECAUSE YOU SEE THEY ALWAYS SINK
BUT NOBODY SAYS "POOR LAD" OR GOES ABOUT LOOKING SAD
BECAUSE YOU SEE IT'S THE WAR, IT'S THE UNALTERABLE LAW.

ALTHOUGH IT'S PERFECTLY CERTAIN THE PILOTS GONE FOR A BURTON
AND THE OBSERVER TOO, IT'S NOTHING TO DO WITH YOU
AND IF THEY BOTH SHOULD GO, TO A LAND, WHERE FALLS NO RAIN
NOR HAIL, NOR DRIVEN SNOW, DO YOU SUPPOSE THEY CARE

YOU AND HERALD, I CRY OR SAY A PRAYER OR SIGH,
IN THE COLD SEA, IN THE DARK, IT ISN'T A LARK
BUT IT ISN'T ORIGINAL SIN IT'S ONLY A "BEAU" GOING IN.

Gavin Ewart

'When a Beau goes in' – poem by Gavin Ewart on the Strike Wing Memorial. (Photo: John Tuck)

Association, conducted by the Chaplain of RAF Coningsby, and attended by the Vice Lord Lieutenant of Lincolnshire, the Mayor of Cleethorpes, current and former RAF personnel, others involved in local aviation heritage, and members of the public.

A Place in History

Bomber bases such as Scampton and Waddington are well-known today, and the Lancaster aircraft that flew from them is legendary. Fighter bases like Biggin Hill and Duxford survive as well-known heritage destinations, and examples of the Hurricanes and Spitfires that were based there, and still fly today, are reminders of the valour of the aircrews and ground crews who served there.

In contrast, the part played by North Coates and its Strike Wing was rarely reported during the war itself, and the significance of Coastal Command generally and the anti-shipping campaign in particular have been overlooked since by military historians. The history of RAF North Coates deserves to be recognised and remembered. In the first half of the war, the squadrons based there flew dangerously unsuitable and out-dated aircraft on anti-shipping operations that frequently verged on the suicidal. From early 1943 onwards, however, the Strike Wing's Beaufighters successfully attacked the enemy's convoys, and gradually closed the North Sea to German shipping.

Unfortunately, there is no Beaufighter flying today, and the aircraft is largely forgotten, although there are Beaufighters on display in museums, including an excellent example of the TFX at the RAF Museum in Hendon. A Beaufighter is being restored privately at Duxford Airfield, the aviation outstation of the Imperial War Museum, with the long-term aim of returning it to flying condition. This survivor of the almost six thousand 'Beaus' that were produced is not a variant used by the Strike Wing squadrons, but when restored it can still serve as a reminder of the anti-shipping role played by this gallant aircraft, and as a memorial to all of the Strike Wing crews who flew them.

Dick Vimpany

Torbeau Navigator, 'A' Flight, 254 Squadron, 1943/45

Dick Vimpany was born in Rugby, Warwickshire, in 1923, and educated at Lawrence Sheriff Grammar School. At school he was one of a group of friends who formed a cadet corps, with a view to enlisting when the time came for this. Among this group were Freddy Hinks, also to become a Navigator with 254 Squadron, and John Nunneley, author of '*Tales from the King's African Rifles*', who served with that regiment in Burma.

Dick left school in 1939, aged 16, to become an apprentice radio engineer, later starting a part-time electrical engineering course for a London University B.Sc. He also joined the RAF Volunteer Reserve. His RAF training proper began in 1941, aged 18, when he entered the service as an aircrew cadet (aircraftman), training first as a wireless operator, at Cranwell. This was followed by training at No. 4 Observers School at West Freugh in Scotland, learning navigation, bomb aiming, air photography and air gunnery, in Anson aircraft. He was then sent to No. 3 School of General Reconnaissance at RAF Squires Gate near Blackpool, for training in ancient Botha aircraft. Having qualified as an Observer, with the rank of Sergeant, he was posted to No 2 Coastal Command Operational Training Unit (OTU) at Catfoss in Yorkshire, where he flew in Beaufighters for the first time. He was originally nominated to fly with Canadian pilot Carl Caldwell, who was killed shortly afterwards in a separate flying accident. Dick then 'crewed up' with an experienced pilot, Squadron Leader Fred Gardiner. Having been selected to fly Torbeaus, they were sent to the Torpedo Training Unit (TTU) at Castle Kennedy, near Stranraer in Scotland, for the final phase of training. When this was completed, they joined 254 Squadron, arriving at North Coates on 1 May 1943, and flew their first operation on 17 May.

Dick Vimpany and Fred Gardiner flew together until Gardiner was posted away from 254 Squadron in April 1944, having been awarded the DFC. Vimpany then flew as a 'spare' navigator with several other pilots, including F/Lt. Don Ford DFC on the Strike of 15 June 1944 off Borkum (Ford was killed in September 1944). He also flew several sorties with W/Cdr. Paddy Burns DFC, CO of 254

Dick Vimpany aged 20 relaxing at the Pestle and Mortar pub in Grimsby in 1943. (Photo: Vimpany archive)

Squadron, hunting E-Boats in the English Channel around D-Day, when Burns' regular navigator was unavailable. Dick Vimpany was commissioned as a Pilot Officer in December 1943.

Vimpany was 'rested' in August 1944, having flown on 45 operational sorties during the most intensive period of the North Coates Strike Wing's campaign. He was then attached for a short period to 157 General Reconnaissance Wing, before returning to 254 Squadron as an intelligence officer in the operations room, where he remained until the end of the war in Europe.

In the closing days of the war he accompanied the Wing on its brief deployment to Helmond in Holland for the 'rampage' over the Kattegat, although he did not fly on those sorties. For some reason that is unclear, on the day after the German surrender on Luneberg Heath he flew to Luneberg, returning to England the following day with a group of liberated RAF POWs. He was promoted to Flight Lieutenant before being demobilised in early 1946.

In the summer of 1944 Dick married Pat Walker, who was serving in the Auxiliary Territorial Service (ATS). They had met when he was billeted at St Annes-on-Sea while training at Squires Gate. After leaving the RAF, now married and with a child, he could not return to an apprenticeship or take up a university place and so turned to civil charter flying as an expedient. He used his £100 'demob' grant plus payment of fees to study and qualify for his civil air navigator and wireless operator licenses. Working for various precariously financed air transport companies, he carried refugees from India to Pakistan and vice versa during the Partition of 1947, flew for months on the Berlin Airlift of 1948, and flew general freight across Europe, Asia and Africa. The aircraft were mainly former RAF Dakotas and converted Lancasters. It was an uncertain way of life, mostly away from home and family, and his children can recall the long absences and the small frugal flats that were home. A far cry from the comforts enjoyed by today's commercial aircrew, this was however the way of life for many demobilised RAF personnel in the late 1940s. Unsurprisingly, many former aircrew took some years to find their feet in the post-war world. Few complained, counting themselves as lucky to have survived. There was no support system, and they were never asked if they suffered anxieties or regrets – but they were resilient. Thankfully, although leading a sometimes precarious existence in the commercial aviation industry, Dick Vimpany was fine.

After grounding himself and qualifying as an air traffic controller, in 1952 he decided to re-join the RAF in order to provide a more secure future or his family. His postings in the RAF were varied and interesting. These included a tour as station navigation officer at RAF Negombo in Ceylon from 1954 to 1956; working to establish the Army Air Corps helicopter capability; and trialling the introduction of the Wessex helicopter into service at RAF Odiham. In the mid-1960s he was deployed for a year (unaccompanied) on active service in Borneo during the 'confrontasi' with Indonesia, working with 51 Gurkha Infantry Brigade to plan and control the movement of helicopter-borne troops and special forces. For this tour of distinguished service, he was awarded the MBE (Military).

Dick Vimpany meets fellow 254 Squadron veteran Arnold Kelshall and his wife Helen in Trinidad in 1966; Kelshall had been shot down and taken prisoner in 1944, but Dick Vimpany believed him to have been killed, so this brief reunion twenty-two years later was a happy surprise. (Photo: Vimpany archive)

His pre-retirement task was to lead an RAF training flight through the Caribbean in 1966. This included visiting Trinidad, where he met up unexpectedly with Arnold Kelshall, a Trinidadian pilot and friend from 254 Squadron, whom he had last seen twenty-two years earlier, shortly before Kelshall was shot down on a Strike in April 1944, believed killed. However, Kelshall had ditched successfully and was taken prisoner. He was now a senior lawyer in Trinidad and the two flyers took the opportunity to reminisce about their wartime experiences, photographed for the national newspaper.

Retiring from the RAF in 1966, Dick Vimpany then spent 17 years as a senior operational scientist at the Ministry of Defence Aircraft Experimental Establishment at Boscombe Down, a fitting conclusion to a career in military aviation for a man with a mathematical and logical mind.

Dick Vimpany remained in contact with a number of his wartime colleagues and attended several Wing reunions, sometimes with Freddie Gardiner. While some of his fellow Strike Wing aircrew were not necessarily strangers to difficult adjustments and some hard times in the early post-war days, most had established themselves successfully in civilian life. A younger guest at the Wing's final reunion at North Coates in 1988 reported that although more than forty years had passed since their final Strike, they had not lost the ability to enjoy a party.

Writing five decades after the end of the war, Dick provided some insight into what had motivated him and his friends and colleagues during their time at North Coates:

> All aircrews in the RAF were volunteers. We did not intend to lose the war – there was too much at stake, for all the world. Throughout the war I never heard once any suggestion that we should not continue fighting. I don't suppose that any of us wanted to fly against the convoys except for one reason – to force the convoys off the seas, which we did. Morale at North Coates was always good. There was sadness when our friends did not return, but we did as we were told.

Dick Vimpany was a young man like many thousands of others, who served their country in its hour of need. He was fortunate to survive. Many of his friends did not. This book is a tribute to Dick and to all of those who served with him in the North Coates Strike Wing; and especially those who *Failed to Return*.

Squadron Leader R.N. Vimpany MBE died in 2006.

Appendix I

Bristol Beaufighter

The Beaufighter airframe design and most of its components were derived from the pre-war Bristol Beaufort. A prototype first flew in July 1939 and the Beaufighter Mark 1 entered service as a home defence night fighter in August 1940. With a crew of two, a pilot and a navigator who also served as wireless operator and rear gunner, the 'Beau' evolved through many variants into one of the most versatile and effective combat aircraft of the Second World War. In total, over 5,900 Beaufighters were manufactured in Britain and Australia.

The first type used by the Strike Wings was the VIC ('C' standing for Coastal), later replaced by the TFX (the TF denoting 'Torpedo Fighter').

Variants deployed by North Coates Strike Wing: June 1942–May 1944[1]

Squadron	Type	From	To
236	VIC	June 1942	July 1943
	TFX	July 1943	May 1945
143[a]	IIF	December 1942	March 1943
	XIC	March 1943	August 1943
	TFX	February 1944	October 1944
254	VIC	June 1942	October 1943
	XI	October 1943	January 1944
	TFX	January 1944	May 1945

a On detachment, so not at North Coates August 1943- February 1944

Armament

Aircraft of 236 and 143 Squadrons, deployed and armed for the anti-flak role, were equipped with six wing-mounted .303 machine guns and four nose-mounted 20mm cannon. The navigator was also equipped with a .303 rear-firing machine gun. From early summer 1943 rocket projectiles (RP) were also introduced for the anti-flak aircraft – two racks of four rockets on each wing.

---

1   See Nesbit, *The Strike Wings*, p.254 and Janes *'All the Worlds Aircraft, 1945-46'*.

The variants flown by 254 Squadron, known as 'Torbeaus', were equipped to carry and launch the new gyroscopically-controlled 18' torpedo armed with a 550lb torpex warhead. The Torbeaus were also armed with nose-mounted cannon, plus the navigator's machine gun.

The Beaufighter offered much flexibility and, in addition to their main strike role, aircraft of all three squadrons were required to carry out various other operations including armed reconnaissance and air-sea searches. Aircraft would be armed and equipped according to the demands of the sortie.

Dimensions	Wingspan 57 ft 10in
	Length 41 ft 4 in
Power Plant	Beaufighter VIC – Two 1,650 hp Bristol Hercules engines
	Beaufighter TFX – Two 1,772 hp Bristol Hercules engines
Performance	Cruising speed approx. 200 mph at 1,000 ft.
	Maximum speed 320 mph at 10,000 ft in level flight; up to 350 mph at sea level.
Range	Approx. 1,500 miles with a drop tank; approx. 1,000 miles with a torpedo

Appendix II

Coastal Command Structure

Coastal Command was one of the three Commands formed in 1936 when the RAF underwent a major restructuring (the other two being Bomber Command and Fighter Command).

Coastal Command was responsible for developing the strategy to deliver the objectives set for the Command by Air Staff, for making the case for resources to be allocated to the Command in order to implement the strategy, and for deploying these resources as effectively as possible.

Commanders-in-Chief, Coastal Command	Appointed
Air Marshal Sir Philip Joubert de la Ferté	September 1936
Air Marshal Sir Frederick Bowhill	August 1937
Air Chief Marshal Sir Philip Joubert de la Ferté	June 1941
Air Marshal Sir John Slessor	February 1943
Air Chief Marshal Sir William Sholto Douglas	January 1944

Coastal Command's home-based operations were divided into Groups, each having specific geographical responsibilities (*see Map on page 14*). North Coates Strike Wing formed part of 16 Group, whose Headquarters were at Chatham, alongside the headquarters of the Royal Navy's Nore Command. Operations were generally initiated and planned at Group level, with orders being passed down to station commanders, for execution by squadron commanders. Group was also responsible for collating intelligence and coordinating joint operations with other Commands.

Air Officers Commanding, 16 Group	Appointed
Group Captain R. L. G. Marix	March 1939
Air Vice-Marshal J. H. S. Tyssen	January 1940
Air Vice-Marshal I. T. Lloyd	February 1942
Air Vice-Marshal B. E. Baker	July 1942
Air Vice-Marshal F. L. Hopps	July 1943

At the start of 1943, 16 Group consisted of fifteen squadrons based at six stations, each commanded by a station Commander. North Coates was one of these six stations.

Station Commanders, North Coates	Appointed
W/Cdr. E.H. Sparling	December 1939
Group Captain J.M. Mason	March 1940
Group Captain F.L. Pearce	March 1942
Group Captain N.C. Ogilvie-Forbes	August 1942
Group Captain P.F. Canning	October 1942
Group Captain O.I. Gilson	April 1943
Group Captain F.J. Braithwaite	January 1944

Each squadron was commanded by a Wing Commander, and consisted of two flights of roughly equal number, each usually commanded by a Squadron Leader. The Squadron COs of the Strike Wing squadrons when these were based at North Coates were as follows:

236 Squadron (designation MB) Commanding Officers	Appointed
W/Cdr. H.D. Fraser (killed)	November 1942
W/Cdr. H.N.G. Wheeler	November 1942
W/Cdr. W.H. Cliff	September 1943
W/Cdr. P.D.F. Mitchell	March 1944
W/Cdr. E.W. Tacon (shot down, taken prisoner)	August 1944
W/Cdr. D.G. Hall	September 1944

254 Squadron (designation QM) Commanding Officers	Appointed
W/Cdr. R.E.X Mack	November 1942
W/Cdr. C.S. Cooper (killed)	April 1943
W/Cdr. A.W.D. Miller	September 1943
W/Cdr. R.E. Burns	January 1944
W/Cdr. D.L. Cartridge	September 1944

143 Squadron (designation NE)	Appointed
W/Cdr. W.O.V. Bennett (killed)	December 1942
W/Cdr. R.N Lambert	June 1943
W/Cdr. E.H. McHardy	February 1944

Appendix III

254 Squadron - Aircrew list, April 1943

Notes made by Dick Vimpany 40 years later

Nominal Roll for 254 Squadron in April 1943

- Sgt Perkins & F/O Savage killed (on Air-Sea search) 5/4/43
- F/Sgt Parsons & F/Sgt Yeates killed 15/4/43
- Sgt. Jack Simpson (NZ) attended Reunion October 1987
- Sgt. (Dave) Pengelly (Canada)
- Sgt. (Lofty) Richardson (Australia) – RNV's pilot on several occasions later
- Sgt. 'Chota' Tatham – Trained with RNV at 4 Air Observers School, West Freugh
- Sgt. Freddy Hinks – At Lawrence Sheriff School, Rugby, one year senior to RNV
- W/Cdr. Patrick Gibbs – See 'The Ship Busters' (and other books) (Authors' note: although appearing on this Roll, Gibbs never took command of 254 Squadron.)
- F/Lt. John Lown & F/Sgt Daynton. Shot down into N. Sea and as far as I know were lost. Lown spotted two days running in a dinghy, which was empty on day 3. (Authors' note ; this was in 1944 when Lown and Daynton had left 254 Squadron.)
- F/Sgt. Ron Garton killed with Sgt Owens 22 June 1943

Appendix IV

Coastal Command: Number of vessels sunk or damaged, April 1940–May 1945

	Total Ships		Total Tonnage		Average Tonnage	
	Sunk	Damaged	Sunk	Damaged	Sunk	Damaged
1940	6	14	5,561	47,662	927	3,404
1941	28	20	51,965	84,367	1,856	4,218
1942	26	20	55,430	82,112	2,132	4,106
1943	32	5	84,759	27,118	2,649	5,424
1944	170	39	183,192	127,258	1,078	3,263
1945	104	36	131,429	144,937	1,264	4,026
Total	366	134	512,336	513,454	1,400	3,832

Source: *Air Historical Branch*, Table E from Goulter Table 3, p.353.

North Coates Strike Wing Squadron

Total surface ships sunk

		Merchant Ships		Surface Warships		Total	
		Ships	Tonnage	Ships	Tonnage	Sunk	Tonnage
1943	Q1	0	0	0	0	0	0
	Q2	5	22,231	5	2,801	10	25,032
	Q3	1	2,700	2	864	3	3,564
	Q4	2	12,660	1	92	3	12,752
1944	Q1	4	11,492	1	150	5	11,642
	Q2	4	9,329	15	15,557	19	24,886
	Q3	5	5,512	47	42,034	52	47,546
	Q4	0	0	6	1,263	6	1,263
1945	Q1	0	0	0	0	0	0
	Q2	4	15,314	1	50	5	15,364
Totals		25	79,238	78	62,811	103	142,049
Averages			3,170		805		1,379

Source: Compiled from Nesbit, Appendix III; excludes U-boats & midget submarines.

List of merchant ships sunk

Date	Ship	Tonnage	Flag	Squadrons
18 April 1943	*Hoegh Carrier*	4,906	Norway	143, 236, 254
29 April 1943	*Aludra*	4,930	Netherlands	143, 236, 254
	Narvik	4,251	Sweden	
17 May 1943	*Kyphissia*	2,964	Germany	143, 236, 254
13 June 1943	*Stadt Emden*	5,180	Germany	143, 236, 254
2 August 1943	*Fortuna*	2,700	Germany	143, 236, 254
23 November 1943	*Weissenburg*	6,316	Germany	236, 254
18 December 1943	*Pietro Orseolo*	6,344	Italy	248, 254
1 March 1944	*Maasburg*	6,415	Netherlands	143, 236, 254
5 March 1944	*Diana*	1,878	Sweden	254, 415
29 March 1944	*Hermann Schulte*	1,305	Germany	143, 236, 254
	Christel Vinnen	1,894	Germany	
20 April 1944	*Storfors*	898	Sweden	143, 236, 254
26 April 1944	*Luise Leonhardt*	4,816	Germany	143, 236, 254
	Lasbek	2,159	Germany	
6 May 1944	*Eduard Geiss*	1,456	Germany	143, 236
8 July 1944	*Tannhauser*	1,923	Germany	236, 254, 144, 404
	Sif	1,437	Sweden	
	Miranda	736	Germany	
8 August 1944	*Vim*	1,221	Norway	254, 455, 489
8 September 1944	*Hengelo*	195	Netherlands	236, 254, 455, 489
3 May 1945	*Dorpat*	3,535	Germany	236, 254
	Inster	4,747	Germany	
	Pallas	627	Germany	
	Taifun	6,405	Germany	
Total	25	79,238		

Source: *Nesbit,* Appendix III.

List of Maps

Bibliography & Sources

The National Archives (TNA)

AIR 15 series:
> Dispatches on the Operations of Coastal Command by Air Chief Marshalls Sir Frederick Bowhill, Sir Philip Joubert de la Ferté and Sir John Slessor.
> Beaufighter Wing at North Coates: operational policy.
> Coastal Command Reviews, 1943-45.

AIR 27 series: Squadron Operations Record Books for 254, 236 and 143 Squadrons.

AIR 28 series: Operations Record Books for North Coates and Appendices.

Books

Aldridge, Arthur, DFC, with Ryan, Mark, *The Last Torpedo Flyers* (London: Simon & Schuster, 2013).

Ashworth, Chris, *RAF Coastal Command, 1936-1969* (London: Patrick Stephens Limited, 1992).

Bird, Andrew D., *A Separate Little War: The Banff Coastal Command Strike Wing Versus the Kriegsmarine and Luftwaffe, 1944-45* (London, Grub Street, 2003)

—— *Heroes of Coastal Command: The RAF's Maritime War 1939-1945* (London: Frontline Books, 2019).

Bowyer, Chas, *Beaufighter at War* (London: Ian Allan Ltd, 1976).

Bridgeman, Leonard, *Jane's All the Worlds Aircraft, 1945-46* (London: Sampson Low, 1946).

Gibbs, Wing Commander Patrick, DSO, DFC & Bar, *Not Peace but a Sword* (London: Grub Street 1993).

—— *Torpedo Leader* (London: Grub Street 2009).

Goulter, Dr Christina J.M., *A Forgotten Offensive: Royal Air Force Coastal Command's Anti-Shipping Campaign, 1940-45* (Abingdon: Frank Cass & Co. Limited, 1995).

Hastings, Max, *Bomber Command* (London, Michael Joseph, 1979).

Kimberley, Bob & Ken, *Home Sweet Home: Wartime Letters of Sergeant Pilot Bob Kimberley* (Exeter: Webb & Bower, 1989).

Nesbit, Roy Conyers, *The Strike Wings* (London: William Kimber & Co. Ltd, 1985).
—— *Coastal Command in Action, 1939–1945* (Stroud: Sutton Publishing Limited, 1997).
Roskill, Captain S.W., DSC, RN, *The War at Sea 1939-1945* (London: HMSO, 1954–61).

Journals

Burns, Group Captain R.E., 'Anti-Shipping Strikes 1939–45', *Aerospace Magazine*, February 1979.
Goulter, Dr Christina J.M.,'RAF Coastal Command's Anti-Shipping Operations in North-West Europe. 1940-45', *Royal Air Force Historical Society Journal*, Issue 33, 2005.

Private Collections

Vimpany archive. Logbooks, Letters, Notes and Photographs of the late Dick Vimpany MBE, 254 Squadron, 1943-1945.
Care archive. Logbooks, Notes and Photographs of the late John Care DFC, 254 Squadron 1943-1944.
Stafford, Brian. 'From Bi-plane to Bloodhound', The History of the North Coates RAF Station.
'Darby archive', Personal memoir 'My Way' by Sylvia Darby, a WAAF serving at North Coates 1942-43.
Gardiner/Fleck family papers. Information about the life and career of Freddie Gardiner DFC.
Martin Plummer. 'RAF Donna Nook – a history'.

Royal Air Force North Coates
Roll of Honour

	SQUADRON. 1943			SQUADRON. 1944			SQUADRON
1942			1 Aug	Sgt A.Goldstone.	143	5 July F/s	A.J.Osborne. 236
6 June Sgt	J.C.Black.	415		Sgt C.H.Watts.		18" S/Lt	E.A.Wills, D.F.C.
12" F/s	J.W.Stirling.		26 Aug P/o	K.M.Stewart.		F/o	D.I.N.G.Sinclair.
14" Sgt	E.Thomas.			F/s W.J.Bunting.		20" F/Lt	A.W.Adams. 254
24" F/s	J.A.Ridley.		25 Aug S/Lt	R.A.Ullman.		22" F/s	F.A.J.Button. 236
F/s	R.W.Veit.			P/o R.Davies.		8 Aug S/Lt	R.H.James. 254
Sgt	G.W.Klarner.		26 Aug F/o	W.G.Bonsey.		P/o	B.A.Reynolds.
Sgt	H.A.Clarson.			Sgt J.Bonyer.		11" F/o	P.M.R.G.DeTheux.
28 June F/s	I.W.Garrin.		26 Aug F/o	R.T.Chinery.		F/s	R.E.Mertens.
Sgt	V.P.Whelpley.			W/o W.A.Jefferies.		F/o	W.D.Grant. 236
Sgt	D.Pearce.		27 Aug F/o	I.F.Stamper.	254	13" F/s	G.A.Crow.
Sgt	B.A.Dakin.			F/o R.P.MaGee.		F/s	W.E.Leake.
F/s	J.McCullum.		16 Sep F/s	D.A.Webster.	236	29" F/s	E.J.Wood. 254
Sgt	H.S.Hasleden.			Sgt C.H.Spears.		F/s	R.Boyle.
Sgt	L.H.Latimer.		16 Sep P/o	N.F.Crisp.		30" F/s	D.J.Fitzgerald. 236
Sgt	R.M.Neil.			Sgt C.Mollison.		F/s	R.C.Fitzgerald.
2nd July F/o	G.G.O.James.		28 Sep W/c	G.S.Cooper, D.F.C.	254	7 Sep F/s	R.H.Hall. 254
F/s	A.K.Farnie.			P/o J.M.Kirkup.		F/Lt	H.B.Kelly.
Sgt	G.A.Pearce.		28 Sep F/o	R.E.W.Sams.	236	10" F/s	A.J.Kimberley. 236
Sgt	T.Gibbons.			Sgt L.Smith.		F/s	J.S.Maenee.
3rd July W/o	B.D.R.McComb		13 Oct F/Lt	I.B.Small.		12" F/o	W.B.Wardle.
F/s	M.Bloomfield.			Sgt A.S.Bissett.		12" F/o	H.R.Dowding. 254
Sgt	R.M.Ennis.		19 Oct P/o	G.H.Martele.		F/o	P.N.Hemy.
Sgt	J.H.LaBelle.			F/s J.A.Mallinson.		23" F/Lt	D.R.O.Ford.
21st Sept W/o	J.A.Bowrasse, R.C.A.F.	236	4 Nov F/s	H.Brennand.		F/o	A.J.Wilcox.
F/s	W.L.Williams.			Sgt H.Macaulay.		28" F/o	R.W.Shepherd.
20 Oct S/Lt	G.R.MacDonald, N.Z.		5 Nov F/o	W.G.Palmer.	254	F/o	W.J.Knowles.
F/o	A.Kerr.	H.Q.16 Group		F/o P.W.S.Smallwood.		5 Oct S/Lt	S.R.Muller-Rowland, D.F.C.&Bar 256
23rd Oct F/o	F.B.Williams.	236	5 Nov Sgt	D.F.Brown.		F/o	A.J.Kendall.
P/o	D.G.Wilmer.			Sgt J.A.Thompson.		15" F/s	J.Williams. 254
Capt	R.C.L.Morgan, Free French.		8 Nov F/s	A.G.Hall.	236	F/s	W.H.Stevens.
Sgt	A.Vuilleumier.			Sgt C.H.Robbins.		8 Nov F/Lt	G.A.Marshall.
7 Nov Sgt	D.G.Lewis.	143	23 Nov F/o	A.F.Hague.	254	F/o	F.Roberts.
20 Nov F/o	R.R.Sargent.	254		F/o H.C.Pavitt.		21" Sgt	J.Dalley.
Sgt	C.Heskel.			F/o N.A.Hattersley.		F/o	G.J.Burns.
20 Nov S/Lt	G.A.Edney.	256		Sgt R.W.Lenton.		27" F/o	T.McAleese.
F/s	H.Haddow.			F/s R.J.O'Connor.		P/o	F.B.Shaw.
W/c	H.D.Fraser, O.B.E.			F/s E.G.Kirkland.		2 Dec W/o	J.W.Howie.
F/o	R.S.Griffin.		23 Nov F/s	J.G.Potter.	236	F/s	F.E.Peet.
26 Nov Sgt	H.G.J.Middleton.			Sgt F.G.Williamson.		28" F/s	P.G.Lamb. 256
P/o	K.G.V.Brown.		11 Dec F/o	T.Sowerbutts.	254	29" F/o	A.J.Stringer. 254
1943				Sgt H.N.Pepper.		29" F/o	J.A.Dunning.
25 Jan F/Lt	T.H.Carson, D.F.C.	254	1945				
P/o	G.E.Bell.		1944			7 Jan W/o	E.J.Prince. 256
27 Jan S/Lt	W.E.L.Lewis.	236	6 Jan Sgt	J.D.McDermid.	254	F/s	C.F.Welstead.
P/o	A.H.A.Treadwell.			Sgt D.B.Rhodes.		17" F/Lt	P.Sutehall.
Sgt	J.B.Wallis.		26 Jan F/s	D.J.Lowe.	236	F/o	A.K.Holvey.
Sgt	C.Murray.		26 Jan F/s	S.B.Wheatley.	254	17" F/o	R.L.Middlemas, D.F.C.
5 Feb F/s	A.A.Mackenzie.	254	26 Jan F/s	M.Yates.	254	W/o	J.Dugdale.
F/s	H.J.Knight.			F/s B.S.Tugwell.		17" P/o	F.P.Troutman. 254
6 Feb W/o	J.H.Clark.	236	28 Jan F/s	W.A.Lynch.	236	P/o	N.Evans.
F/s	R.Eadie.			F/s W.A.Jukes.		17" F/s	A.J.Maton.
16 Feb F/Lt	J.G.Stephenson.	254	7 Feb F/Lt	J.F.Acer. R.C.A.F	415	17" F/o	G.D.Warburton.
F/s	T.W.D.White.			W.O.2 J.L.Dissing, R.C.A.F.		F/o	J.A.Grey.
27 Mar F/s	S.L.Guernon, Free French	236		W.O.2 C.J.McCarvill, R.C.A.F.		F/s	R.J.Rothwell.
5 Apr F/o	M.Savage.	254		W.O.2 N.C.West. R.C.A.F.		11 Mar F/s	R.B.Steward.
Sgt	L.G.Perkins.			W.O.1 C.E.Simpson,R.C.A.F.		21" F/s	E.G.Langley.
9 Apr L.A.C.	C.H.J.Payne.	S.H.Q		W.O.1 E.J.Dorval. R.C.A.F.		W/o	D.P.O'Donoghue. 236
15 Apr F/o	S.Parsons.	254		W.O.2 J.E.Russell. R.C.A.F.		F/s	K.Allen.
F/s	A.W.Yeate.		8 Feb S/Ldr	M.W.Gibson, R.C.A.F.		14 Apr F/s	D.R.Newman. 254
29 Apr F/o	J.H.Wilsdon.	143		F/o O.A.Lamb. U.S.A.A.F.		F/s	K.D.Wall.
Sgt	H.Thompson.			W.O.2 A.R.Armitage. R.C.A.F.		F/s	H.J.Nicholson.
1 May F/s	J.G.W.Foster.			F/s R.McGillivray, R.C.A.F.		7" F/s	P.J.Fulton.
Sgt	B.Girnuck.			F/o E.Hanson. R.C.A.F.		F/s	J.Scott.
S/Lt	E.G.Pett, D.F.C.	254		W.O.2 J.L.A.Champoux,R.C.A.F.		F/s	M.K.Farrington.
F/s	R.J.Crossley.			F/s R.Urban. R.C.A.F.		1944	
F/s	F.Poore.		1944			20 Apr LT.	R.J.Niven. 143
Sgt	K.D.Jones.		16 Feb F/s	J.L.Mallon.	254	F/o	W.T.Davy.
Sgt	S.S.Marshall.			Sgt R.P.Crawford.		23 Apr F/o	R.Agnew.
Sgt	K.J.Highstead.		21 Feb F/s	G.G.A.Caron. Free French	618	11" F/s	H.B.Blackwell.
7 May F/o	J.R.Worswick.	143	23 Feb F/s	J.G.Pollard.		F/s	F.G.Newport.
F/s	L.M.Smith.			P/o R.Barr.	236	F/s	J.M.Slater.
13 May Sgt	R.Davidson.	7 A.A.C.U.		F/o F.Jones.		12 Sep LT.	D.C.Cormack.
24" F/s	A.J.Hebblewhite.		23 Feb F/s	R.H.Sharp.	143	F/o	J.Stanners.
F/s	J.A.Williams.			F/s F.R.Bennett.		17" Sgt	W.J.Jones.
13 June S/Lt	P.J.E.Ritchie, D.F.C.		7 Mar F/o	E.L.Walker.	254	25 Sep P/o	W.N.Auld.
F/o	E.W.Marsden.			F/s E.T.Helps.		F/s	G.T.Oldbury.
22 June F/s	R.C.Garton.		24 Mar F/s	E.H.Smith.		F/o	D.L.Cameron.
Sgt	M.E.Owens.			F/s J.McPherson.		F/o	M.Marwood.
2nd" W/c	W.O.V.Bennett, D.F.C.A.F.C	143	24 Mar P/o	H.W.Platten.	236		
F/o	H.Emmerson.			F/o R.H.Johnson.			
27" F/o	J.B.Mann, R.C.A.F.		20 Apr W/o	L.W.Marshall.			
Sgt	G.E.Wilson.			Sgt M.Kerr.			
12 July F/o	A.R.Welch.	256	20 May Cpt	P.L.Mendousse.			
F/s	P.Crawforth.			F/o M.W.Hushwick.			
16" F/o	M.E.Lawton.	143	6 June S/Lt	R.L.Hanbury.	254		
F/o	A.P.Stevenson.			F/o W.Ogston.			
18" F/o	A.P.Blackie.		13" F/s	E.W.Preston.	236		
F/o	R.N.Farrow.			F/s S.F.Cooper.			
" F/s	E.F.V.Kidd.	236		F/o R.West.			
Sgt	H.C.Stevenson.		5 July F/s	K.R.Mead, D.F.M.			

Located in Cleethorpes Town Hall. (Photo: John Tuck)

This was truly our finest generation